Comparative Literature

To Clive, who forced me to stop talking long enough to sit down and write.

Comparative Literature

A Critical Introduction

Susan Bassnett

BLACKWELL
Oxford UK & Cambridge USA

First published 1993

Blackwell Publishers
108 Cowley Road
Oxford OX4 1JF
UK

238 Main Street
Cambridge, Massachusetts 02142
USA

British Library Cataloguing in Publication Data
A CIP catalogue record for this book is available from the British Library.

Library of Congress Cataloging-in-Publication Data
Bassnett, Susan.
  Comparative literature: a critical introduction/Susan Bassnett.
    p. cm.
  Includes bibliographical references and index.
  ISBN 0–631–16704–8. – ISBN 0–631–16705–6 (pbk.)
    1. Literature, Comparative – History and criticism. 2. Literature, Modern – 20th century – History and criticism. 3. Criticism.
I. Title.
PN865B37 1993
809'. 04048 – dc20   92–45856
                                                                 CIP

Typeset in 11 on 12½ pt Sabon
by Best-set Typesetters
Printed in Great Britain by TJ Press Ltd, Padstow Cornwall
This book is printed on acid-free paper

Contents

Acknowledgements

A great many people have helped with the creation of this book. I am grateful to my students over the past sixteen years at the University of Warwick, who have taught me so much about comparing cultures and have made me constantly aware of the gaps in my own knowledge. To some of those students especially, my debt is particularly great: Karin Littau, Hasnah Ibrahim, John Dixon, Gisela Funk deserve special mention. Else Veira, who introduced me to the work of Brazilian translation theorists, has been invaluable. My colleagues, Piotr Kuhiwczak and Sabina Sharkey have offered help and advice whenever needed, and ideas that have gone into the writing of this book have been discussed with Tony Phelan, John Stokes, John Rignall and Keith Hoskin, special friends and colleagues all. The manuscript was splendidly typed as ever by Irene Renshaw, assisted in the final stages by Chris Richley and Val Melling. Particular thanks to Stephan Chambers at Blackwell, who has been patient and supportive throughout.

This book, like my previous ones, has been made possible by a lot of help from other women: the staff of the University of Warwick creche, the helpers at Wolvey village playgroup, Marlene Lawler, my mother, Eileen Bassnett, my daughters Lucy, Vanessa and Rosanna. My son Luke has been no help at all, but his presence in my life is a continual joy. Finally, my thanks to Clive Barker, to whom this book is dedicated.

Introduction: What is Comparative Literature Today?

Sooner or later, anyone who claims to be working in comparative literature has to try and answer the inevitable question: What is it? The simplest answer is that comparative literature involves the study of texts across cultures, that it is interdisciplinary and that it is concerned with patterns of connection in literatures across both time and space.

Most people do not start with comparative literature, they end up with it in some way or other, travelling towards it from different points of departure. Sometimes the journey begins with a desire to move beyond the boundaries of a single subject area that might appear to be too constraining, at other times a reader may be impelled to follow up what appear to be similarities between texts or authors from different cultural contexts. And some readers may simply be following the view propounded by Matthew Arnold in his Inaugural Lecture at Oxford in 1857 when he said:

> Everywhere there is connection, everywhere there is illustration. No single event, no single literature is adequately comprehended except in relation to other events, to other literatures.[1]

It could almost be argued that anyone who has an interest in books embarks on the road towards what might be termed comparative literature: reading Chaucer, we come across Boccaccio; we can trace Shakespeare's source materials through Latin, French, Spanish and Italian; we can study the ways in which Romanticism developed across Europe at a similar moment in time, follow the process through which Baudelaire's fascination with Edgar Allan Poe enriched his own writing, consider how many English novelists

learned from the great nineteenth-century Russian writers (in translation, of course), compare how James Joyce borrowed from and
loaned to Italo Svevo. When we read Clarice Lispector we are
reminded of Jean Rhys, who in turn recalls Djuna Barnes and Anaïs
Nin. There is no limit to the list of examples we could devise. Once
we begin to read we move across frontiers, making associations and
connections, no longer reading within a single literature but within
the great open space of Literature with a capital L, what Goethe
termed *Weltliteratur*. Goethe noted that he liked to 'keep informed
about foreign productions' and advised anyone else to do the same.
'It is becoming more and more obvious to me,' he remarked, 'that
poetry is the common property of all mankind.'[2]

At this juncture, one could be forgiven for assuming that comparative literature is nothing more than common sense, an inevitable
stage in reading, made increasingly easier by international market-
ing of books and by the availability of translations. But if we
shift perspective slightly and look again at the term 'Comparative
Literature', what we find instead is a history of violent debate that
goes right back to the earliest usage of the term at the beginning of
the nineteenth century and continues still today. Critics at the end
of the twentieth century, in the age of post-modernism, still wrestle
with the same questions that were posed more than a century ago:
What is the object of study in comparative literature? How can
comparison be the object of anything? If individual literatures
have a canon, what might a comparative canon be? How does the
comparatist select what to compare? Is comparative literature a
discipline? Or is it simply a field of study? These and a great many
other questions refuse to go away, and since the 1950s we have been
hearing all too frequently about what René Wellek defined as 'the
crisis of Comparative Literature'.[3]

Comparative literature as a term seems to arouse strong passions,
both for and against. As early as 1903, Benedetto Croce argued
that comparative literature was a non-subject, contemptuously
dismissing the suggestion that it might be seen as a separate
discipline. He discussed the definition of comparative literature as
the exploration of 'the vicissitudes, alterations, developments and
reciprocal differences' of themes and literary ideas across literatures,
and concluded that 'there is no study more arid than researches of
this sort'. This kind of work, Croce maintained, is to be classified 'in
the category of erudition purely and simply'.[4] Instead of something

called comparative literature, he suggested that the proper object of study should be literary history:

> the comparative history of literature is history understood in its true sense as a complete explanation of the literary work, encompassed in all its relationships, disposed in the composite whole of universal literary history (where else could it ever be placed?), seen in those connections and preparations that are its raison d'être.[5]

Croce's argument was that the term 'comparative literature' was obfuscatory, disguising the obvious, that is, the fact that the true object of study was literary history. Considering the pronouncements on comparative literature made by scholars such as Max Koch, founder and editor of the two German comparative journals, *Zeitschrift für vergleichende Literatur* (1887–1910) and *Studien zur vergleichenden Literaturgeschichte*(1901–9), Croce claimed he could not distinguish between literary history pure and simple and comparative literary history. The term, 'comparative literature', he maintained, had no substance to it.

But other scholars made grandiose claims for comparative literature. Charles Mills Gayley, one of the founders of North American comparative literature, proclaimed in the same year as Croce's attack that the working premise of the student of comparative literature was:

> literature as a distinct and integral medium of thought, a common institutional expression of humanity; differentiated, to be sure, by the social conditions of the individual, by racial, historical, cultural and linguistic influences, opportunities, and restrictions, but, irrespective of age or guise, prompted by the common needs and aspirations of man, sprung from common faculties, psychological and physiological, and obeying common laws of material and mode, of the individual and social humanity.[6]

Remarkably similar sentiments to those expressed in 1974 by François Jost, when he claimed that 'national literature' cannot constitute an intelligible field of study because of its 'arbitrarily limited perspective', and that comparative literature:

represents more than an academic discipline. It is an overall view of literature, of the world of letters, a humanistic ecology, a literary Weltanschauung, a vision of the cultural universe, inclusive and comprehensive[7]

Such claims go far beyond the methodological and shed some light on quite why the debate on comparative literature should have been so bitter. For Jost, like Gayley and others before him, are proposing comparative literature as some kind of world religion. The underlying suggestion is that all cultural differences disappear when readers take up great works; art is seen as an instrument of universal harmony and the comparatist is one who facilitates the spread of that harmony. Moreover, the comparatist must possess special skills; Wellek and Warren in their *Theory of Literature*, a book that was enormously significant in comparative literature when it first appeared in 1949, suggest that:

> Comparative Literature ... will make high demands on the linguistic proficiencies of our scholars. It asks for a widening of perspectives, a suppression of local and provincial sentiments, not easy to achieve.[8]

The comparatist is here depicted as someone with a vocation, as a kind of international ambassador working in the comparative literatures of united nations. For Wellek and Warren go on to state that 'Literature is one; as art and humanity are one'. It is an idealistic vision that recurs in the aftermath of major international crises; Goethe could confidently (and quite wrongly) assert in 1827 that 'national literature means little now', and Wellek and Warren offered the cultural equivalent of the movement towards a United Nations Assembly that was so powerfully felt in the aftermath of the Second World War.

The high ideals of such a vision of comparative literature have not been met. A decade after *Theory of Literature* appeared, Wellek was already talking about the crisis in comparative literature and even as the subject appeared to be gaining ground in the 1960s and early 1970s, flaws in the idea of universal values and of literature as one could already be seen. The great waves of critical thought that swept through one after the other from structuralism through to post-structuralism, from feminism to deconstruction, from semiology to psychoanalysis – shifted attention away from the activity of comparing texts and tracking patterns of influence between writers towards the role of the reader. And as each new wave broke over the preceding one, notions of single, harmonious readings were shattered forever.

In the 1950s and early 1960s, high-flying graduate students in the West turned to comparative literature as a radical subject, because at that time it appeared to be transgressive, moving as it claimed to do across the boundaries of single literature study. That there was no coherent methodology did not matter, nor did it matter that the debates on whether the subject existed or not still continued unabated from the previous century. 'We spend far too much of our energy talking . . . about Comparative Literature and not enough of it comparing the literature,' complained Harry Levin in 1969, urging more practical work and less agonizing about the theory.[9] But Levin's proposal was already out of date; by the late 1970s a new generation of high-flying graduate students in the West had turned to Literary Theory, Women's Studies, Semiotics, Film and Media Studies and Cultural Studies as the radical subject choices, abandoning Comparative Literature to what were increasingly seen as dinosaurs from a liberal – humanist prehistory.

Yet even as that process was underway in the West, comparative literature began to gain ground in the rest of the world. New programmes in comparative literature began to emerge in China, in Taiwan, in Japan and other Asian countries, based, however, not on any ideal of universalism but on the very aspect of literary study that many western comparatists had sought to deny: the specificity of national literatures. As Swapan Majumdar puts it:

> it is because of this predilection for National Literature – much deplored by the Anglo-American critics as a methodology – that Comparative Literature has struck roots in the Third World nations and in India in particular.[10]

Ganesh Devy goes further, and suggests that comparative literature in India is directly linked to the rise of modern Indian nationalism, noting that comparative literature has been 'used to assert the national cultural identity'.[11] There is no sense here of national literature and comparative literature being incompatible.

The work of Indian comparatists is characterized by a shift of perspective. For decades, comparative literature started with Western literature and looked outwards; now what is happening is that the West is being scrutinized from without. Majumdar points out that what Indian scholars call western literature, regardless of geographical precision, includes those literatures which derive from Graeco-Roman matrices via Christianity, and he terms English, French, German, etc. as 'sub-national literatures'. It is quite clear that what he is bringing to comparative literature, in the terms in which he uses it, is a radically alternative perspective and a revaluation of the discourse of 'national' literature. Accustomed as those of us in the West are to thinking in terms of 'great' literatures, of 'majority' versus 'minority' literatures, the Indian perspective as articulated by Majumdar is a startling one. Homi Bhabha sums up the new emphasis in an essay discussing the ambivalence of post-colonial culture, suggesting that:

> Instead of cross-referencing there is an effective, productive cross-cutting across sites of social significance, that erases the dialectical, disciplinary sense of 'Cultural' reference and relevance.[12]

Developments in comparative literature beyond Europe and North America do indeed cut through and across all kinds of assumptions about literature that have come increasingly to be seen as Eurocentric. Wole Soyinka and a whole range of African critics have exposed the pervasive influence of Hegel, who argued that African culture was 'weak' in contrast to what he claimed were higher, more developed cultures, and who effectively denied Africa a history. James Snead, in an essay attacking Hegel, points out that:

> The outstanding fact of late twentieth-century European culture is its ongoing reconciliation with black culture. The mystery may be that it took so long to discern the elements of black culture already there in latent form, and to realize that the separation between the cultures was perhaps all along not one of nature, but one of force.[13]

What we have today, then, is a very varied picture of comparative literary studies that changes according to where it is taking place. African, Indian, Caribbean critics have challenged the refusal of a great deal of Western literary criticism to accept the implications of their literary and cultural policy. Terry Eagleton has argued that 'literature, in the meaning of the word we have inherited, *is* an ideology,'[14] and he discussess the way in which the emergence of English as an academic subject in the nineteenth century had quite clear political implications. The establishment of the subject in the universities, he maintains, followed the vast social changes brought about in the aftermath of the first World War:

> The Great War, with its carnage of ruling class rhetoric, put paid to some of the more strident forms of chauvinism on which English had previously thrived . . . English Literature rode to power on the back of wartime nationalism; but it also represented a search for spiritual solutions on the part of the English ruling class whose sense of identity had been profoundly shaken . . . Literature would be at once solace and reaffirmation, a familiar ground on which Englishmen could regroup both to explore, and to find some alternative to, the nightmare of history.[15]

Eagleton's explanation of the rise of English ties in with the aspirations of many of the early comparatists for a subject that would transcend cultural boundaries and unite the human race through the civilizing power of great literature. But just as English has itself entered a crisis (what, after all, is English today? Literature produced within the geographical boundaries of England? Of the United Kingdom? Or literatures written in English from all parts of the world? And where does the boundary line between 'literature' on the one hand and 'popular' or 'mass' culture on the other hand lie? The old days when English meant texts from *Beowulf* to Virginia Woolf are long gone, and the question of what to include and exclude from an English syllabus is a very vexed one); so also has Comparative Literature been called into question by the emergence of alternative schools of thought. The work of Edward Said, pioneer of the notion of 'orientalism', has provided many critics with a new vocabulary. Said's thesis, that

> the Orient was a word which later accrued to it a wide field of meanings, associations and connotations, and that these did not necessarily refer to the real Orient but to the field surrounding the word[16]

provides the basis for essays such as Zhang Longxi's 'The Myth of the Other: China in the Eyes of the West', in which it is argued that 'for the West, China as a land in the Far East becomes traditionally the image of the ultimate Other'.[17] The challenge posed by non-European critics to the colonizing nations' systematic process of 'inventing' other cultures has put ideology firmly back on the agenda of literary studies.

A European or North American literature syllabus could, until fairly recently, concern itself primarily with an established canon of great writers. But a syllabus devised in a non-European culture, particularly in one which underwent a period of colonization by a Western power, has to tackle completely different issues. Hence the vexed question of Shakespeare in India, for example, a canonical writer hailed in the nineteenth century as the epitome of English greatness. Indian students have the problem therefore of dealing with Shakespeare not only as a great figure in European literature, but also as a representative of colonial values: two Shakespeares, in effect, and in conflict with one another. One way of tackling this problem is to treat Shakespeare comparatively, to study the advent of Shakespeare in Indian cultural life and to compare his work with that of Indian writers.

The growth of national consciousness and awareness of the need to move beyond the colonial legacy has led significantly to the development of comparative literature in many parts of the world, even as the subject enters a period of crisis and decay in the West. The way in which comparative literature is used, in places such as China, Brazil, India or many African nations, is constructive in that it is employed to explore both indigenous traditions and imported (or imposed) traditions, throwing open the whole vexed problem of the canon. There is no sense of crisis in this form of comparative literature, no quibbling about the terms from which to start comparing, because those terms are already laid down. What is being studied is the way in which national culture has been affected by importation, and the focus *is* that national culture. Ganesh Devy's argument that comparative literature in India coincides with the rise of modern Indian nationalism is important, because it serves to remind us of the origins of the term 'Comparative Literature' in Europe, a term that first appeared in an age of national struggles, when new boundaries were being erected and the whole question of national culture and national identity was under discussion throughout Europe and the expanding United States of America. In chapter 2 we shall be looking more closely at the process of development of both the term and the subject.

It is possible to argue that as we come to the end of the twentieth century, we have entered a new phase in the troubled history of comparative literature. That the subject is in crisis in the West is in no doubt, though it is interesting to speculate on what will happen as the former Eastern European states revise their syllabuses, for they are living through a phase of nationalism that has long since disappeared in the capitalist Western states. Falling student numbers, the uneasiness of many comparatists that is revealed in defensive papers or a reluctance to engage in definition of what exactly their subject consists of, the apparent continuation of the old idea of comparative literature as binary study, i.e., as the study of two authors or texts from two different systems (though the problem of how to define different systems is a complex one and unresolved), all these factors reinforce the picture of a subject that has lost its way, even as courses in literary theory and post-colonial theory proliferate and publishers' catalogues list books in these areas under separate headings. But equally, it is also apparent that the subject is expanding and developing in many parts of the world where it is explicitly linked to questions of national culture and identity. Comparative literature as it is being developed outside Europe and the United States is breaking new ground and there is a great deal to be learned from following this development.

Whilst comparative literature in the Third World and the Far East changes the agenda for the subject, the crisis in the West continues. The new comparative literature is calling into question the canon of great European masters, and this process coincides with other challenges – that of feminist criticism, which has questioned the male orientation of cultural history; and that of post-modernist theory, which revalues the role of the reader and, through the work of writers such as Jacques Derrida and Pierre Bourdieu, has exposed the part played by the subterranean forces of institutionalized power structures, masquerading as centres of universal liberalism.

Significantly, however, Western readers are approaching these challenges without recourse to something called 'Comparative Literature'. The rush of books on post-colonial literature at the start of the 1990s reflects a new interest in this hitherto neglected area of study. The opening statements of *The Empire Writes Back*

(subtitled: Theory and Practice in Post-Colonial Literatures) include the following phrases: 'the term "post-colonial" . . . is most
appropriate as the term for the new cross-cultural criticism which
has merged in recent years and for the discourse through which
this is constituted.'[18] What is this but comparative literature under
another name?

Another rapidly expanding development in literary studies, and
one which has profound implications for the future of comparative
literature, is 'translation studies'. Since the early usage of this term
in the mid-1970s, the subject has developed to such an extent
(through publishing, conferences, the establishment of Chairs in
universities, research programmes, etc.) that there are many now
who consider it to be a discipline in its own right. What distinguishes
translation studies from translation as traditionally thought of, is its
derivation from the polysystems theory developed by Itamar Evan-
Zohar and later by Gideon Toury in Tel Aviv.[19] Translation studies
will be discussed in more detail later in this book, but essentially the
key to its rapid expansion and successful entry into literary studies
lies in its emphasis on literature as a differentiated and dynamic
'conglomerate of systems', characterized by internal oppositions
and dynamic shifts. This notion of literature as a polysystem sees
individual literary systems as part of a multi-faceted whole, thereby
changing the terms of the debates about 'majority' and 'minority'
cultures, about 'great' literatures and 'marginal' literatures. Moreover, translation studies derives from work in linguistics, literary
study, history, anthropology, psychology, sociology and ethnology
among others, and posits the radical proposition that translation is
not a marginal activity but has been and continues to be a major
shaping force for change in the history of culture. Comparative
literature has traditionally claimed translation as a sub-category,
but this assumption is now being questioned. The work of scholars
such as Toury, Lefevere, Hermans, Lambert and many others has
shown that translation is especially significant at moments of
great cultural change. Evan-Zohar argues that extensive translation activity takes place when a culture is in a period of transition: when it is expanding, when it needs renewal, when it is in a
pre-revolutionary phase, then translation plays a vital part. In
contrast, when a culture is solidly established, when it is in an
imperialist stage, when it believes itself to be dominant, then
translation is less important. This view explains why, in simple

terms, the emergent European nations in the early nineteenth century, those engaged in struggles against the Austro-Hungarian or Ottoman Empires, translated so enthusiastically, and why translation into English began to decrease as the British Empire extended its grasp ever further. Later, as English became the language of international diplomacy in the twentieth century (and also the dominant world commercial language), there was little need to translate, hence the relative poverty of twentieth-century translations into English compared with the proliferation of translations in many other languages. When translation is neither required nor wanted, it tends to become a low status activity, poorly paid and disregarded, and the implications of this process have come increasingly to be studied by people working in the field of translation studies, which effectively offers a new way of looking at cultural history, taking into account both the implications of socio-historical changes that affect literary production in different cultures and the linguistic structuring of a text as it is transported across language boundaries. It may well be, as is suggested in chapter 7 below, that we need to reassess the role of translation studies vis-à-vis comparative literature, for whilst comparative literature in the West seems to be losing ground, even as it becomes more nebulous and loosely defined, so translation studies is undergoing the opposite process. Just as it became necessary for linguistics to rethink its relationship with Semiotics, so the time is approaching for comparative literature to rethink its relationship with Translation Studies. Semiotics was at first regarded as a sub-category of linguistics, and only later did it become clear that the reverse was the case, and linguistics was in effect a branch of the wider discipline, semiotics. Comparative literature has always claimed translation as a sub-category, but as translation studies establishes itself firmly as a subject based in inter-cultural study and offering a methodology of some rigour, both in terms of theoretical and descriptive work, so comparative literature appears less like a discipline and more like a branch of something else. Seen in this way, the problem of the crisis could then be put into perspective, and the long, unresolved debate on whether comparative literature is or is not a discipline in its own right could finally and definitely be shelved.

1

How Comparative Literature Came into Being

First Appearance of the Term

There is general agreement that comparative literature acquired its name from a series of French anthologies used for the teaching of literature, published in 1816 and entitled *Cours de littérature comparée*. In an essay discussing the origins of the term, René Wellek notes that this title was 'unused and unexplained'[1] but he also shows how the term seems to have crept into use through the 1820s and 1830s in France. He suggests that the German version of the term, 'vergleichende Literaturgeschichte', first appeared in a book by Moriz Carrière in 1854, while the earliest English usage is attributed to Matthew Arnold, who referred to 'comparative literatures' in the plural in a letter of 1848.[2]

Regardless of whether named individuals can be credited with having introduced the term into their own languages, it is clear that some concept of 'comparative literature' which involved a consideration of more than one literature was in circulation in Europe in the early years of the nineteenth century. The term seems to have derived from a methodological process applicable to the sciences, in which comparing (or contrasting) served as a means of confirming a hypothesis.

In his inaugural lecture at the Athénée in 1835, entitled *Littérature étrangére comparée* (Foreign Literature Compared), Philaréte Chasles endeavoured to define the object of study in the following terms:

> Let us calculate the influence of thought upon thought, the manner in which the people are mutually changed, what each of them has given, and what each of them has received; let us calculate also the

effect of this perpetual exchange upon the individual nationalities: how, for example, the long-isolated northern spirit finally allowed itself to be penetrated by the spirit of the south; what the magnetic attraction was of France for England and England for France; how each division of Europe has at one time dominated its sister states and at another time submitted to them; what has been the influence of theological Germany, artistic Italy, energetic France, Catholic Spain, Protestant England; how the warm shades of the south have become mixed with the profound analysis of Shakespeare; how the Roman and Italian spirit have embellished and adorned the Catholic faith of Milton; and finally, the attraction, the sympathies, the constant vibration of all these living, loving, exalted, melancholy and reflected thoughts – some spontaneously and others because of study – all submitting to influences which they accept like gifts and all in turn emitting new unforeseeable influences in the future![3]

A key word in that text is 'influence', and indeed the study of influences has always occupied an important place in Comparative Literature. Chasles also refers to the 'spirit' of a nation or of a people, and suggests that it is possible to trace how that spirit may have influenced another writer in another culture. He paints an idealistic picture of international literary harmony, suggesting that stereotypes may have some basis in historical reality but insisting on the mutuality of influences and connections.

Culture and Nationalism

But Chasles' idealistic picture of international cooperation, of influences being brought, like gifts from one culture to another, is only half the story. There was another, completely different notion of cultural exchange. Byron was aware of this alternative perspective as early as 1819, when in the Preface to his *Prophecy of Dante* he commented that:

The Italians with pardonable nationality, are particularly jealous of all that is left them as a nation – their literature, and in the present bitterness of the classic romantic war, are but ill-disposed to permit a foreigner even to approve or imitate them, without finding some fault with his ultramontane presumption.[4]

What Byron could see, of course, was the close relationship between national identity and cultural inheritance, and he was shrewd enough to recognize that a nation (or series of small states, as Italy then was) engaged in struggles for independence jealously guarded its literary heritage against all comers. The fine line between influence perceived as borrowing and influence perceived as appropriation or theft was very much a matter of perspective.

In an essay discussing the role played by translated literature in the Czech literary revival of the first half of the nineteenth century, Vladimír Macura stresses the politics of translation, since translation has always played such a key role in patterns of influence.[5] He cites Josef Jungmann, revolutionary scholar and patriot, who claimed in 1846 that 'in the language is our nationality'. Jungmann saw translation as a significant part of the development of the new Czech literature, and argued that the point of origin of a text was less important than what happened to that text in the process of translation. In Jungmann's vision, translation into Czech was a process of enhancement, a means of extending the range of the language and of the emergent literature. Clearly for a culture searching for its roots or for a culture struggling for its independence from foreign occupation, the question of influences was a heavily-charged one and by no means innocent.

In general terms, it is possible to see the late eighteenth and early nineteenth centuries as a time of immense literary turmoil throughout Europe, as issues of nationality increasingly appeared linked to cultural developments. Nations engaged in a struggle for independence were also engaged in a struggle for cultural roots, for a national culture and for a past. The need to establish antecedents became vital; emergent nations had to establish a tradition and a canon, and probably the most extraordinary example of the search for roots is the case of the forged medieval manuscripts 'discovered' by Vaclav Hanka. In 1817–18, Hanka and his colleagues announced their discovery of unique manuscripts in Old Czech from the ninth, tenth and thirteenth centuries, evidence that proved conclusively that there had been a golden age of Czech poetry at a time when the rest of Europe was still struggling with the decayed epic form. Later, it was revealed that the manuscripts were fraudulent, but by then such a powerful impulse had been given to Czech literature that this exposure barely mattered. After centuries of repression, Czech had been seen to be a major European language, with a present *and* a past. Between 1822 and 1827 three volumes of Slavonic National Songs were published, the first part of František Palacky's five volume *History of Bohemia* appeared in 1836, and in the same year Karel Macha, the greatest poet of the Czech Romantic revival, published his major poem, *May*.

The case of the forged medieval manuscripts that so assisted the Czech National revival is probably the most extreme example of the desperate desire to establish cultural roots as part of an ongoing cultural and political struggle. But the tendency to look back to a glorious hidden past was shared by peoples throughout Europe. The period from the mid-eighteenth century onwards saw an intense interest in the publication of folk songs, and poetry and fairy tales. Percy's *Reliques of Ancient English Poetry* appeared in 1765, Johannes Ewald, the great Danish poet, published a significant collection based on ancient sagas and medieval ballads in 1771, Herder's *Stimmen der Volker in Lieder* came out in 1778, Jakob and Wilhelm Grimm's *Fairy Tales* appeared in 1812–13 and Elias Lonnrot's version of the finnish national epic, the *Kalevala*, appeared in 1849. This fascination with the past, matched by developments in literary history, philology, archaeology and political history was linked to the general European question of definitions of nationhood. Rousseau talked about the collective personality of 'the people', and as Timothy Brennan points out:

> In Germany, Herder transformed Rousseau's 'people' into the *Volk*. The significance of this latter concept is its shift from Rousseau's Enlightenment emphasis on civic virtue to a woollier Romantic insistence on the primordial and ineluctable roots of nationhood as a *distinguishing feature* from other communities. Each people was now set off by the 'natural' characteristics of language, and the intangible quality of a specific *Volksgeist*.[6]

The idea of a cultural heritage that sprang from the people, from the 'genuine', 'authentic' voices of the collective upon which the nation was based, was a very powerful one in the age of revolutions that swept Europe. Not all emergent nations invented their own non-existent medieval literature, but it is significant that a key text which caught the public imagination right across Europe and was translated into a huge range of languages was also a forgery – James Macpherson's *Fingal*, which appeared in 1762.

The Impact of Ossian

Macpherson claimed that his poem was a translation of a Gaelic epic by the ancient Irish bard, Ossian (Ois(n)). *Fingal* was such a success that Macpherson went on to 'translate' other epics. He had already produced, in 1760, a collection of poetry purported to have been collected in the Highlands of Scotland, but his version of Ossian surpassed everything else he produced. Frederic Lolliée described Ossian later, in *A Short History of Comparative Literature from the Earliest Times to the Present Day* (1906), as 'a northern Dante, as great and majestic, and no less supernatural than the Dante of Florence, more sensitive than he and more human than the singer of the *Iliad*.'[7] The poems of Ossian, forgeries though they were, proved to be sensationally popular. The subject matter combined romance, heroism, accounts of mythical lands and savage lyricism probably derived from folk versions of the extant Ossianic poems, and Macpherson must have had a good knowledge of ancient Gaelic poetry in the first instance in order to be able to produce his forgeries.

Scholars have endlessly discussed both the impact of Macpherson's work in different literary systems, such as the French, the Italian, the Polish or the Czech, and speculated on reasons for the success of the Ossian poems. Certainly, it is significant that Macpherson remains a set text on the curriculum of English departments in many parts of the world today, ranking alongside Byron as an author of fundamental importance in the late eighteenth and early nineteenth centuries. In contrast, he is unknown to the vast majority of students of English literature, and in the English-speaking world he appears at best very occasionally as a footnote. This tells us a great deal about the impact of this particular writer upon different literary scenes, and once again it is impossible to divorce the fortunes of Macpherson from the political reality of his age. Dr. Johnson accused him of forgery from the outset, but it is not on account of his forgeries that he is not taught in Britain, just as the fact of his forgeries has nothing to do with his place in the Italian or Polish canons of English Literature respectively. Rather, Macpherson's success (and lack of it) can be traced to the role played by his texts in the debate on national culture and national identity that was being so hotly discussed throughout Europe. In Britain, where Scottish and Irish nationalism were both feared and despised, there was a vested interest in denying the possibility of a great bardic past to those cultures. In other nations seeking to establish their identity there was a powerful drive towards rediscovering the past felt by many scholars, writers and ordinary people and in this, combined with the drive to translate the best of other nations' literature, there also seems to have been an urge to satisfy a hunger for culture.

The Imperial Perspective

The picture changes radically, when we turn to consider the way in which Europe was projecting itself on the rest of the world. The American revolution of 1776 had set the native English of the colonists off along a new road, and in the early nineteenth century the revolutions in Latin America were to follow a similar process of rupture with Spain. The vexed question as to whether an author like Ann Bradstreet could be considered American (because she lived and wrote in New England for most of her life) or English (because her poems were published in England, there not being facilities available in the colonies) could finally be resolved. American literature may have taken English writers as models, but American writers were developing separately, in terms of means of production as well as subject matter and form. Likewise, through the nineteenth century we find Latin American writers endeavouring to create an epic fit for a new continent, still caught up in the coils of publishing policy, censorship, stylistic constraints and a host of other legacies from Spain and Portugal, but nevertheless seeing revolutionary struggle as linked to the emergence of new literatures.

Literary developments in the New World reflected a new order. In complete contrast is the attitude of a colonial power to the literature produced by peoples under its domination, and probably the most extreme example of this philistine vision is the (in)famous comment by Macaulay, who, in 1835, stated that:

> I have never found one among them (Orientalists) who could deny that a single shelf of a good European library was worth the whole native literature of India and Arabia. I have certainly never met with any Orientalist who ventured to maintain that the Arabic and Sanscrit poetry could be compared to that of the great European nations.[8]

Lord Macaulay's attack on the cultural heritage of the Middle East and the Indian subcontinent strikes us today as both racist and absurd, yet the underlying assumptions of Macaulay's position were widely shared. Edward Fitzgerald, whose translation of the *Rubáiyát of Omar Khayyám* became one of the great classic poems of the nineteenth century also had a low opinion of Oriental literature. 'It is an amusement to me,' he wrote to his friend Cowell on March 20, 1857, 'to take what liberties I like with these Persians, who, (as I think) are not Poets enough to frighten one from such excursions and who really do want a little Art to shape them.'[9]

Belief in the superiority of their own culture was a part of the politics of imperialism. The rhetoric which dismissed African or Asian peoples as 'primitive' or 'childlike' also dismissed their art forms in various ways. Oral culture was generally regarded as being of lower status, so the existence of a tradition of oral epics, for example, was considered insignificant. At the same time, because of the importance of the written epic in the European tradition, those cultures which had no epic and which saw the lyric as the highest form of poetry were also downgraded. Homer and the Greeks, the plays of Shakespeare, the poetry of Spenser and Milton, these were the texts against which other works were measured and found wanting.

Once again, the crux of the problem was one of perception. The Shakespeare that was taken to India was a writer who was depicted as being the embodiment of English virtue and virtuosity. Shakespeare the great master, Shakespeare the supreme English writer, Shakespeare the epitome of Englishness was what came to be exported. The existence of an alternative picture, the revolutionary poet whose plays about the deposition of unjust rulers were staged across Europe in cities seethingwith revolutionary energy, was not permissable. And with the exportation of the idealized Shakespeare came all the evils of colonialism, which led Jawaharlal Nehru to draw an ironic contrast between what he called 'the two Englands':

> Which of these two Englands came to India? The England of Shakespeare and Milton, of noble speech and writing and brave deed, of political revolution and the struggle for freedom, of science and technical progress, or the England of the savage penal code and brutal behaviour, of entrenched feudalism and reaction? For there were two Englands, just as in every country there are these two aspects of national character and civilization.[10]

Men like Macaulay, liberal intellectuals with a genuine belief in the superiority of their own culture and a vision of the world that involved strict hierarchies based on class, race and colour were also engaging in comparison. The problem was that they inevitably compared negatively. Some literatures were worth less than others, some were unique in having universal importance and others could be disregarded as primitive or banal. The question of the universal value of an author or a work was fundamental to this colonialist viewpoint, for it enabled claims to be made that set works apart from all other considerations, arguing that a writer such as Shakespeare, for example, was on a higher plane than almost anyone else. The basis for claims of universality tended, as they still do, to argue for some kind of common transcultural sharing of emotional experience, and disregarded the vicissitudes of literary history. So the fact that Ben Jonson was considered to be a greater writer than Shakespeare by his contemporaries and by subsequent generations for well over a century after his death was ignored. By the time Shakespeare was being exported to India and the other colonies in the mid-nineteenth century, his compatriots regarded his universal greatness as a matter of fact, not speculation, and the process of discovering Shakespeare that had gone on through the eighteenth century was disregarded completely.

Cultural colonialism was also a form of comparative literature, in that writers were imported by the colonizing group and native writers were evaluated negatively in comparison. Of course such practices were never described as comparative literature, for comparatists through the nineteenth century kept insisting that comparison took place on a horizontal axis, that is, between equals. One result of this perspective was that from the beginning, comparative literature scholars tended to work only with European writers. The prevalence of this attitude is attested by the fact that it has still not disappeared in the minds (and syllabuses) of many contemporary comparatists. In 1967, for example, C. L. Wrenn gave the Presidential Address of the Modern Humanities Research Association in Chicago (and then again in London two weeks later) entitled *The Idea of Comparative Literature*, in which he suggested that:

Clearly fundamental differences in patterns of thinking among peoples must impose relatively narrow limits. An African language, for example, is incompatible with a European one for joint approaches in Comparative Literature study. Even Sanskrit, though itself an Indo-European language along with its Indian ramifications, presents a pattern of thought which renders any sort of literal translation of very limited value.[11]

He goes on to say that a comparative study of *Paradise Lost* and the *Ramayana*, for example, can only discuss parallels and differences in subject matter and treatment at the expense of the poetry, and suggests that this is inevitable because of the different nature of Sanskrit thought and feeling. The only proper object of study for comparatists, he argues, is 'European languages, medieval or modern'.

Nat'l idea → comp Lit

The Paradox of Early Comparative Literature

The term 'comparative literature' appeared in an age of transition. In Europe, as nations struggled for independence – from the Ottoman Empire, from the Austro-Hungarian Empire, from France, from Russia – and new nation states came into being, national identity (whatever that was) was inextricably bound up with national culture (however that was defined). Later comparatists may have chosen to ignore the heated political context in which the first statements about comparative literature were made, but it is striking to note that even whilst ideas of universal literary roots were being discussed, along with ideas about the spirit or soul of a nation, comparisons were being made that involved evaluating one culture higher than another. 'France is the most sensitive of all countries . . . what Europe is to the world, France is to Europe,' said Philarète Chasles in his 1835 speech to the Athénée, adding also that he had 'complete contempt for narrow-minded and blind patriotism'.[12] This double vision enabled him to make claims for the unbiased nature of comparative literature, whilst simultaneously proclaiming French superiority.

Lord Macaulay's attitude when he consigned Indian and Arabian literatures to the scrapheap was not unlike Chasles', for he too had an absolute belief in the superiority of his own culture. Both were products of the Europe of their time, recognizing the inter-relatedness of European literary systems and what Chasles termed 'the part of other nations in the grand civilizing movement', but perceiving that which came from outside Europe as alien. Even Goethe's remarks about 'world literature' need to be seen in context, for although he eventually turned his attention to the literatures of continents beyond Europe, his coinage of the term 'Weltliteratur' related to his views on Europe and in particular to his desire for an end to war.

What becomes apparent when we look at the origins of comparative literature is that the term predated the subject. People used the phrase 'comparative literature' without having clear ideas about what it was. With the advantages of retrospection, we can see that 'comparative' was set against 'national', and that whilst the study of 'national' literatures risked accusations of partisanship, the study of 'comparative' literature carried with it a sense of transcendence of the narrowly nationalistic. In other words, the term was used loosely but was associated with the desire for peace in Europe and for harmony between nations. Central to this idealism was also the belief that comparison could be undertaken on a mutual basis. So Chasles in 1835 and Abel François Villemain in 1829 hailed the value of studying patterns of influence, listing the names of great writers from a variety of different countries. Comparative literary study, according to Chasles, was to be before anything else, a 'pleasure trip', involving a look at great figures from the sixteenth century onwards. Communication, comingling, sharing were key words in this view of comparative literature, which depoliticized writing and aspired towards universal concord. Comparative literature seems to have emerged as an antidote to nationalism, even though its roots went deep into national cultures. Chasles and Villemain could discuss the greatness of past writers with urbanity and scholarly distinction, but they were primarily Frenchmen and their interest focused on the 'gift-giving' process of literary influences between France and its neighbours. Likewise, the enormous interest throughout Europe in the early nineteenth century for Byron and Shakespeare, as evidenced by the proliferation of translations of their works, was not so much due to an interest in England and English culture, but rather due to the use that could be made of two writers who could be read as prototypical revolutionaries. The idea that there was mutuality in comparison was a myth, yet it was a myth as profoundly believed as the myth of universal, transcultural greatness.

Given the ambiguities surrounding the origins of the term, it is hardly surprising that comparative literature scholars from the

mid-nineteenth century onwards should have been almost obsessively concerned with defining their subject. Ulrich Weisstein says
that either Jean-Jacques Ampère, author of *Histoire de la littérature
française au moyen age comparée aux littératures étrangères* (1841)
or Abel FrançoisVillemain, author of *Tableau de la littérature au
moyen age en France, en Italie, en Espagne et en Angleterre* (2
vols, 1830) 'must be regarded as the true father of a systematically
conceived Comparative Literature in France – or anywhere, for that
matter'.[13] Conceiving systematically something that had come into
being so loosely was no easy matter. What Villemain and Ampère
did was to write what could be described as histories of literatures,
showing patterns of connection and influence. It was not until
later in the century that Chairs of Comparative Literature were
established, and the subject acquired academic status. The first
Chair was set up in Lyon in 1897 and subsequently other Chairs
appeared in France. French comparative literature dominated the
field, with other European countries much slower in establishing
Chairs. In the United States, however, Charles Chauncey Shackwell
taught a course in 'general or comparative literature' at Cornell
from 1871 onwards, and Charles Mills Gayley taught comparative literary criticism at the University of Michigan from 1887, while
the first Chair in the subject was established at Harvard in 1890.
Indeed, it is in the last two decades of the nineteenth century that
Comparative Literature began to be established internationally, for
in addition to the subject being taught in institutions of higher
education in Europe and the United States, Hutcheson Macauley
Posnett, Professor of Classics and English Literature at University
College, Auckland, New Zealand, published a full length study of
the subject, entitled *Comparative Literature* in 1886, and two
journals were founded in Europe. The first, set up in 1879 by Hugo
Meltzl de Lomnitz, a German speaking scholar from Cluj in what
is now Rumania, was a multilingual publication, entitled *Acta
comparationis litterarum universarum*. This was followed by two
periodicals edited by the German scholar Max Koch, *Zeitschrift
für vergleichende Literaturgeschichte* (1887–1910) and *Studien zur
vergleichenden Literaturgeschichte* (1901–1909).

Throughout the nineteenth century, use of the term 'comparative
literature' was flexible. Self-styled comparatists followed the principle outlined by Humpty Dumpty, who points out to Alice that
when he uses a word, 'it means just what I choose it to mean neither

more nor less', though they certainly did not follow his second principle, which was that whenever he used a word a lot he always paid it extra. The term 'comparative literature' drifted into use in several languages, meaning whatever anyone chose it to mean.

Early French studies, such as the works by Ampère and Villemain noted above, focused on the Middle Ages, on that moment in the development of European cultural systems when linguistic boundaries were only loosely drawn and national boundaries were not defined at all, when there was free traffic between scholars and poets. Dante, hailed as father of the Italian language, did, after all, praise the Provençal poet Arnaut Daniel as as his master, granting him the supreme honour of allowing him to speak in his native language in Canto XXIV of *Purgatorio*, and thereby demonstrating that poetry as he conceived it was not tied to native language or culture. The Middle Ages offered a rich field of study for comparatists, because when they turned to a period of European history that was so completely different, they could set aside the vexed questions of their own day, the bitter animosities that so often led to the shedding of blood and which were caused by the drawing of frontiers according to political rather than geographical or ethnographical criteria. Yet later French comparatists questioned the legitimacy of studying the Middle Ages, arguing that only post-medieval literature was the proper province of comparative enquiry. The influential critic Paul Van Tieghem proclaimed in 1931 that:

> Comparative Literature comprises the mutual relations between Greek and Latin literature, the debt of modern literature (since the Middle Ages) to ancient literature, and, finally, the links connecting the various modern literatures. The latter field of investigation, which is the most extensive and complex of the three, is the one which Comparative Literature, in the sense in which it is generally understood, takes for its province.[14]

Van Tieghem's arguments against the study of the Middle Ages reversed the earlier view that the period offered a unique opportunity for comparatists because of the lack of clearly defined boundaries between nations. He proposed instead that modern literatures were best suited to comparative analysis, and he also suggested that the comparison should take place between two elements only. Anything beyond that was not the proper province of comparative literature. It was, in his view, something else altogether.

What happened in the century between the publication of Villemain's two volume study of the Middle Ages in 1830 and Van Tieghem's narrow definition in 1931 continues to affect our understanding of comparative literature today, and it is worth trying to trace the shifts in attitude towards comparative literature that led to Van Tieghem's bold but very limiting book, in which he set oral culture, folklore and pre-Renaissance literature outside the boundaries of his comparative literature and formulated the notion of binary studies that has served the subject so ill for so long.

Attempts at Definition

Readers today, considering France and Germany as the twin giants of the European Economic Community, could be forgiven for overlooking the very different state of affairs that prevailed in the nineteenth century. Moving on beyond both the Revolution and the rise and fall of Napoleon, France by the mid-nineteenth century was a wealthy power with colonies throughout the world, a strong industrial base and a belief in the superiority of its language, institutions and culture. Germany, on the other hand, was an assortment of little states, united by language but striving towards a political centre and in search of a soul. Since, as has been suggested above, comparative literature was linked to nationalism from the start, it is hardly surprising that as a subject it should have developed so differently in France and Germany. The French perspective, which appears as oriented more towards the study of cultural transfer, always with France as either giver or receiver, was concerned with defining and tracing 'national characteristics'. As Ferdinand Brunetière said in 1900:

> the history of Comparative Literature will sharpen in each one of us, French or English, or German, the understanding of the most national characteristics of our great writers. We establish ourselves only in opposing; we are defined only by comparing ourselves to others; and we do not know ourselves when we know only ourselves.[15]

The German perspective, however, was somewhat different. In the introduction to his new journal, *Zeitschrift für vergleichende Literaturgeschichte*, Max Koch praised the achievements of Herder in originating 'a new conception of literature and literary history', arguing that Herder's work on poetry and folksong 'opened up one of the most fertile and extensive areas of comparative literary history'. Koch saw translation as a fundamental area of comparative enquiry, and set German literature and its history as the 'point of departure and the centre of the efforts which the *Zeitschrift* intends to aid'. Folklore, he maintains, has become a discipline in its own right, but nevertheless the comparative study of folksong and poetry is seen as fundamental to comparative literature.[16] We can compare this view to Van Tieghem, who had very definite views on why folklore should be excluded from comparative literature:

> This (the fairy-tale, myth, legend etc.) is folklore and not literary history; for the latter is the history of the human mind viewed through the art of writing. In this subdivision of thematology, however, one considers only the subject matter, its passage from one country to another, and its modifications. Art plays no part in these anonymous traditions whose nature it is to remain impersonal.[17]

It is perhaps not too simplistic to see the keyword in this passage as 'mind', and to reflect that French comparative literature tended more towards the study of the products of the human mind, whereas German comparatists were more concerned with the 'roots' or 'spirit' of a nation. This difference in terminology and in emphasis was due to the different cultural traditions and different political and economic development patterns of France and Germany in the nineteenth century. Those differences became exacerbated in the twentieth century, as French comparatists sought to restrict the use of the term and pin it down, while German comparatists (or some German comparatists) became increasingly chauvinistic. As Ulrich Weisstein puts it, referring to the situation in Hitler's Germany in the 1930s: 'How could Comparative Literature flourish in a country in which the plays of Shakespeare, Molière and Eugene O'Neill were banned from the stage, and where the novels of the great French and Russian writers were no longer accessible?'[18] The journal established in 1877 by Hugo Meltzl de Lomnitz takes a different position, and presents a different case for Comparative Literature. De Lomnitz argued in his editorial statement that the discipline of comparative literature was not yet established, and that the task of his journal was to assist with the process of establishing it. He set out three principle tasks: a revaluation of literary history, which he described as having been relegated to the status of 'the handmaiden' of political history or philology; a revaluation of translation as an art; and a belief in multilingualism. He attacked the chauvinism of comparative literature based on narrowly defined ideas of nationalism:

> it cannot be denied that the so-called 'world literature' is generally misunderstood. For today, every nation demands its own 'world literature' without quite knowing what is meant by it. By now, every nation considers itself, for one good reason or another, superior to all other nations, and this hypothesis, worked out into a complete theory of suffisance, is even the basis of so much of modern pedagogy which today practically everywhere strives to be 'national'.[19]

De Lomnitz's views strike us today as both enlightened and far-reaching. He correctly predicted the significance of translation in the development of comparative literature and argued convincingly for literary history to have an existence in its own right and not as a back-up for some other subject. His concern for multilingualism meant that he took a keen interest in minority languages and literatures, and one of the founding principles of his journal was a belief that the political importance or lack of it of a nation should not intrude upon the comparative study of literatures. Hence a comparison between a Slovene and a French writer might be undertaken on its own terms, with no suggestion that the latter might be worth more than the former simply on account of the status of French literature in the European tradition.

But de Lomnitz's journal had little impact on the development of comparative literature outside Eastern Europe. The French model tended to dominate, though some of the French work was so extreme that we can only look at it with astonishment today. Lolliée's *Short History*, which Weisstein dismissed as obsolete even when it came out in 1903, does nevertheless reflect a particular way of structuring literary history, based on a profoundly chauvinistic viewpoint. Consider, for example, Lolliée's account of English literature at the close of the eighteenth century, the years that saw the publication of works that have come to be looked upon as classic texts:

In England, at the end of the eighteenth century, political agitation was too rampant for the peaceful cultivation of letters amidst the demands of war and public events. Literature, at such times, becomes almost, if not wholly, political . . . imaginative literature declined. History and oratory held the first place; poetry was neglected; yet the century gained in practical activity what it lost in poetic idealism.[20]

Having made this statement, Lolliée has to compensate with a footnote for the names he has left out. He therefore adds that 'it is interesting to note that between 1789 and 1814, among a score of romance writers of some reknown, fourteen were women, three of whom won European reputation, namely, Ann Radcliffe, Maria Edgeworth, and Jane Austen, but especially the two former.'

It seems more likely, considering examples such as the above, that Lolliée's work was largely disregarded by later comparatists because of his ignorance of literary history, rather than on account of his methodology. His book is a good example of the shortcomings of a a particular kind of comparative literature, in which woolly idealism combines with chauvinistic nationalism and the whole is compounded by a grossly over-ambitious project (the history of all literatures) and the writer's own (considerable) lacunae.

Paul Van Tieghem was undoubtably reacting against comparative literature of the Lolliée variety, but in trying to formulate precise boundaries for comparative literature he created a new set of problems. He endeavoured to solve the problem of the term by setting up distinctions between 'comparative' literature, 'general' literature and 'world' literature. In his view, comparative literature should involve the study of two elements (*études binaires*), whilst general literature should involve the study of several literatures. This distinction did not help at all and only added to the confusion, for as René Wellek notes:

> it is impossible to draw a line between Comparative Literature and general literature, between, say, the influence of Walter Scott in France and the rise of the historical novel. Besides, the term 'general literature' lends itself to confusion; it has been understood to mean literary theory, poetics, the principles of literature.[21]

Wellek also points out that comparative literature in the restricted sense of binary relations 'cannot make a meaningful discipline', because it would involve dealing with fragments and could have no methodology of its own. In the chapter entitled 'General, Comparative, and National literature' in a book co-written with Austin Warren (*Theory of Literature*, 1963), René Wellek returns again to the attack, this time suggesting that one of the results of the narrow binary approach has been a decline in interest in comparative literature in recent years.

Certainly the French emphasis on binary studies of Van Tieghem, Fernand Baldensperger and the other French scholars involved in the creation of the *Revue de littérature comparée* in 1921 conditioned several generations of comparatists. Once the problem had been how to determine what might *not* be the province of comparative literature; now exclusion zones were set up according to carefully formulated criteria. Comparative literary study could take place between two languages, so a study involving French and German authors would be acceptable. What would be unacceptable, however, would be a study between two writers working in English, regardless of whether one was Canadian and the other Kenyan. Nor would a study of *Beowulf* and *Paradise Lost* be acceptable, because although the former is in Anglo-Saxon, technically Anglo-Saxon is an early variant of modern English, so part of the same literary system. Van Tieghem took pains to sort out which francophone Belgian or Swiss writers might be included (the ones who tended to gravitate towards Paris), and then excluded those who preferred to remain in their homelands. Comparative literature should study the impact of works by named individuals, hence it was author-centred, and oral literature, anonymous literature and collective or folk literature were outlawed. An enormous amount of time and energy was expended on trying to determine what the boundary lines should be – when was a dialect really a language? When did a nation become a nation – when it had a literature of its own, or when it had a political frontier? When did folk-literature become 'proper' author-based literature? These and a range of other related questions bedevilled comparatists for decades, with French scholars reacting strongly for or against the restrictions and formulating sets of alternatives. It is possible to see almost all French comparative literature from the 1930s onwards as coloured by the *études binaires* principle, by the need some felt to defend it and the impulse which led scholars such as Jean-Marie Carré, Marius François Guyard and René Etiemble to try and move beyond it.

The notion of languages as the fundamental distinction that enabled comparison to take place was probably the most widely accepted principle of all, and as late as the mid-1970s when I was appointed to set up Comparative Literature at Warwick, I had clear instructions at first not to admit English–American comparative projects and to insist on all students having at least two languages. The linguistic distinction as the basis for comparative literature, following the French approach, had become widespread.

The fallacy of that approach is plain to see. Language and culture are inextricably bound together, and a view that sees linguistic boundaries as the principle line to draw for establishing the basis of comparative study is bound to fail. The binary approach never did work; all it succeeded in doing was to restrict the projects comparative literature scholars were allowed to undertake, creating obstacles where none had existed previously and deliberately choosing to ignore other, larger issues. Even someone like Ulrich Weisstein, author of one of the great classic books on comparative literature of our time, is caught up in the coils of binary study and the language problem, so that whilst he can bring himself to admit that there probably is a case for allowing comparative study between English and American literature, since both cultures have 'gone their own ways, at least since the early nineteenth century', he cannot bring himself to admit another kind of distinction: 'It would be . . . questionable to separate, for the sake of a misguided methodological purism, Irish from English literature; for by such a sleight-of-hand writers like Swift, Yeats and Shaw would be artistically uprooted for the sake of a nonliterary principle.'[22]

That Irish writers may have been included in the English canon in the first place through non-literary principles does not seem to have occurred to Weisstein. He could just about admit to difference between American and English literatures, but that was as far as he could go. To proceed further would be to return to the vexed questions of language, national culture and identity, that ill-defined swampland from which Comparative Literature had first emerged in post-Waterloo France and which subsequent scholars had kept trying to forget.

In his essay, 'The Crisis of Comparative Literature', based on the talk he gave in 1959, René Wellek made a strong attack on what he saw as obsolete methodology and partisan nationalism. He warned that comparative literature had still not established itself properly as a subject on any serious basis, and that it was continuing to wrestle with problems that had long since ceased to have any relevance. He laid the blame on the French school:

> All these flounderings are only possible because Van Tieghem, his precursors and followers conceive of literary study in terms of nine-teenth century positivistic factualism, as a study of sources and influences . . . They have accumulated an enormous mass of paral-lels, similarities and sometimes identities, but they have rarely asked what these relationships are supposed to show except pos-sibly the fact of one writer's knowledge and reading of another writer.[23]

René Wellek was writing over a quarter of a century ago, but his essay can be read today as prophetic. When he accused Van Tieghem and the French group of restricting the scope of comparative literature, of fostering a blinkered approach that led nowhere except into a series of blind alleys, each bearing the names of two possibly obscure writers working in two different languages, he pointed out that such an approach could have obvious con-sequences. In fact, what happened was that subsequent generations of younger scholars turned away from a subject that appeared to be antiquated and irrelevant, and, as has already been suggested in the Introduction, the number of literary theoreticians has expanded whilst the number of comparatists has contracted. There is no place in the post-modernist world for a subject that continues to quibble about whether Yeats should be considered Irish or English and whether a study on the impact of Ibsen on modernist drama can be properly termed 'comparative' or 'general' literature.

The time has come, as René Wellek and Harry Levin were saying long ago, to abandon the old, unnecessary distinctions and to see them for what they were, as the products of a particular age and a particular cultural context. In the next chapter, we shall consider an alternative perspective on comparative literature, also not without its failings, but which can at least be contrasted with the binary approach – the development of comparative literature outside Europe.

2
Beyond the Frontiers of Europe: Alternative Concepts of Comparative Literature

In 1961, in a collection of essays on comparative literature published by the Southern Illinois University Press and edited by Newton Stallknecht and Horst Frenz, Henry Remak attempted to define what he called the 'American school':

> Comparative Literature is the study of literature beyond the confines of one particular country, and the study of the relationships between literature on the one hand, and other areas of knowledge and belief, such as the arts (e.g. painting, sculpture, architecture, music), philosophy, history, the social sciences (e.g. politics, economics, sociology), the sciences, religion, etc., on the other. In brief, it is the comparison of one literature with another or others, and the comparison of literature with other spheres of human expression.[1]

Remak's essay laid out the basis of an American comparative literature that was distinctive from the French school, thereby breaking the power of the French model once and for all. Remak's definition was a summary of trends in practice across the United States and became in effect the manifesto of the American School of comparative literature. He justified himself, stating that he had deliberately chosen an approach that is not historical or generic, but rather descriptive and synchronic. He contrasted his own approach with that of former comparatists and provided an annotated bibliography of volumes of comparative literature. He was well aware of the terminological problem, referring to the 'haziness' of the distinction between comparative and general literature, for example, and agreeing that there is a 'twilight zone where a case can be made pro and con the 'comparativeness' of a given topic'.[2] Remak believed that the French approach was too narrow, and relied too heavily on factual evidence. Influence studies in the French tradition, he argued, were unimaginative, deriving from a positivistic approach, and so he presented an alternative model:

> In a good many influence studies, the location of sources has been given too much attention, rather than such questions as: what was *retained* and what was *rejected*, and *why*, and *how* was the material absorbed and integrated, and with *what success*? If conducted in this fashion, influence studies contribute not only to our knowledge of literary history but to our understanding of the creative process and of the literary work of art.[3]

Remak's wide-ranging definition has been frequently quoted, and not infrequently attacked. While French scholars spent a considerable amount of time and energy trying to confine comparative literature within boundaries, delineating precisely what could and could not be considered proper to the subject, Remak and his colleagues were proposing a definition that deliberately transgressed boundaries. Following Remak and the American school, anything could be compared with anything else, regardless even of whether it was literature or not. Crucial to Remak's argument was the notion that comparative literature should not be regarded as a separate discipline with its own laws, but should rather be seen as an auxiliary discipline, as a bridge between subject areas. His approach centres around the keyword 'process', unlike the French emphasis on 'product'. Faced with the task of laying down rules, he avoids it and shifts the burden of responsibility onto the individual who, he argues, must decide what the bases for comparative study are to be.

One of the bases that Remak avoids is the vexed question of nationalism, and indeed in his definition cited above, he uses the more neutral term 'country' instead. A country can be thought of more in geographical than ideological terms, and so his definition is depoliticized in a very significant way.

The process of depoliticization of comparative literature is a hallmark of the American school, in marked contrast to the development of comparative literature in Europe, and although heavily influenced by New Criticism, it goes back a long way, finding its roots in some of the earlier work in the nineteenth century. Charles Mills Gayley, who set up comparative literature at Berkeley in the 1890s and taught the hugely successful Great Books course that was to serve as a model for future US development, saw his work as quintessentially humanitarian and looked back to a line deriving from Matthew Arnold, via Posnett and Arthur Marsh. He was also well aware of the problems of definition and method, but in his paper entitled 'What is Comparative Literature?' (1903), the clear differences between his approach and the attitude of European scholars can be seen. Gayley proposed that comparative literature should be seen as 'nothing more or less' than literary philology, and formulated an early version of the American school definition, by insisting on the importance of psychology, anthropology, linguistics, social science, religion and art in the study of literature. Distanced from the nationalistic fervour of European states, and the struggles for independence of emergent Latin American nations, Gayley and fellow American comparatists looked instead to a model that involved interdisciplinary work. Literary study was part of a network of related subjects which nourished one another and were part of the organic structure that was Culture. Problems of defining nationhood according to language difference or political boundaries were set aside, and instead what we find is the melting pot theory of comparative literature. Just as the United States prided itself on providing a melting pot for all comers, into which national and linguistic differences would be cast so as to be forged into something new and all-encompassing, so the American perspective on comparative literature was based from the start on ideas of interdisciplinarity and universalism. Scholars argued that study needed to be systematic, but refrained from any further restrictions. Gayley quite openly complained about the term 'comparative literature' itself, which he felt was too slippery and misleading, but could not devise anything that might be adequate as an alternative. Instead, he endeavoured to establish certain principles for the development of the subject, chief of which was a turning aside from the pathway trodden by European comparatists. Gayley even went so far as to challenge one of the fundamental premises of the French school, that is, that comparative literature involved the study of two or more literatures. He pointed out that the study of international relations and influences was one branch of the subject, and that'the study of a single literature may be just as scientifically comparative if it seeks the reason and law of the literature in the psychology of the race or of humanity.'[4]

Gayley's contemporary, Hutcheson Macaulay Posnett, founding father of Antipodean comparative literature, also proposed a non-nationalistic model. His book, *Comparative Literature* came out in 1886, and fifteen years later, in 1901, he published a paper entitled 'The Science of Comparative Literature', in which he reviewed the responses to his book and considered the state of comparative literature as a subject in the English-speaking world. His call for Chairs to be established in comparative literature had gone unheeded in Britain, he noted, though it had been adopted in the United States, and he claimed that despite 'amateur criticism', there had been considerable advances in the field. Posnett's views on comparative literature rested on an evolutionary model, and he proposed that the fundamental principles of the subject were 'social evolution, individual evolution, and the influence of the environment on the social and individual life of man'.[5] The term 'comparative', he suggested, was synonymous with 'historical', but terminology nothwithstanding, the method was the same, and consisted in 'retracing the steps man has taken individually and collectively in reaching the highest social life'.[6]

Posnett's evolutionary model and Gayley's melting pot idealism stand in marked contrast to European versions of comparative literature, and as we try to make sense of the different strands that are still with us today, it is helpful to try and disentangle European approaches from non-European ones. The development of comparative literature in France or Germany or Hungary or Italy ran parallel to socio-political changes, and was always intricately bound up with a sense of the importance of history. In the United States, or in New Zealand where Posnett taught, the priorities were different. In very general terms, we can make a distinction between what could be termed Old World comparative literature – where the emphasis was on sources, on documenting how texts came to be read across cultural and linguistic boundaries, on tracing origins and establishing the cultural basis of national consciousness – and New World comparative literature, where the emphasis was quite different. New World comparatists saw their task in transnational terms; they were concerned with tracing humanity's achievements through time and space, and across disciplinary lines. The question of how to define a national literature was almost irrelevant; instead, what mattered was what Posnett called 'the great moral need' of studying those truths produced by great art.

Avoiding History

It is important to note that contrary to the interpretation of some critics, New World comparative literature was not originally ahistorical. The difference between the Old and the New lay rather in a distinction between ideas of what history was. The evolutionary model accorded well with the forward-looking dynamics of a society freed from nationalistic conflicts, but it was by no means always ahistorical. Arthur Marsh, Professor of Comparative Literature at Harvard in the 1890s, defined his subject in the following terms:

> To examine . . . the phenomena of literature as a whole, to compare them, to group them, to classify them, to enquire into the causes of them, to determine the results of them – this is the true task of comparative literature.[7]

What distinguished the New World approach in the early twentieth century was the absence of partisanship and an idealistic belief in the evolving greatness of human creativity. The problem of ahistoricity came later, for as the American version of the formalist method, through the New Critics, acquired such a firm hold on literary criticism, so questions of history *per se* became less important. Literary history could be considered apart from vexed questions of social, political or economic history, though it is worth noting that Fredric Jameson, in *The Prison-House of Language*, his account of the development of Russian Formalism and Structuralism, draws attention to the differences between Russian and American versions:

> The two movements reflect a more general historical shift in the literary and philosophical climate with the passing of the nineteenth century. This shift, often described as a reaction against Positivism, varies according to the composition of the national and cultural situation in which it takes place, and according to the dominant ideology against which the younger writers rebel.[8]

The shift towards an increasingly formalist model of comparative literature came gradually. At first, as Jameson suggests, it could be seen as a combination of New World idealism with a rejection of positivism, but after 1945 the process accelerated. In 1945, with the end of the Second World War, Europe, the United States and the Commonwealth were forced to reconsider all kinds of previous assumptions. The century that prided itself on its technological advances, on the development of mass communication, improved medical care and an unprecedented rise in the standard of living in the industrialized societies, had nevertheless succumbed to two major wars that had killed millions and that had arisen from nationalist and territorial conflicts unresolved from previous ages. Small wonder that a generation of New World students of comparative literature favoured the idealistic transnational approach of the Great Books model, with its assumptions about the humanizing power of great international art. The object of study was the text; problems of context were consciously left aside. René Wellek sums up this when he proposes that comparative literature

> is identical with the study of literature independent of linguistic, ethnic, and political boundaries. It cannot be confined to a single method ... nor can comparison be confined to actual historical contacts. There may be ... as much value in comparing phenomena such as languages or genres historically unrelated as in studying influences discoverable from evidence of reading or parallels ... The three main branches of literary study – history, theory and criticism – involve each other ... comparative literature can and will flourish only if it shakes off artificial limitations and becomes simply the study of literature.[9]

Wellek, of course, represents the union of the Old with the New, having started out as a European formalist and ended up as the grand old man of American comparative literature. His view is consistent: history is central to comparative literature, but it should be cultural history and not any other kind.

It was this deliberate avoidance of socio-economic or political issues that was eventually to produce a reaction and lead to the birth of New Historicism in North American criticism in the 1970s and 1980s. Trying to compare texts across cultures whilst omitting to look at certain key questions was an enterprise that involved the comparatist in what can only be described as virtuoso tight-rope walking. Irish literature should not be separated from English literature, says Weisstein, because 'by such a sleight of hand' writers like Yeats or Shaw would be 'artistically uprooted for the sake of a nonliterary principle'.[10] A consideration of African literature, he also argues, must examine 'whether a particular world view or a specific local color may be regarded as producing national literary traits'.[11] No mention of the historical perspective here; invasions, colonization, economic deprivation are all set aside, for what is being considered is literature, and only literature, as though all writers worked in a vacuum divorced from external reality.

Post-Colonial Approaches

In complete contrast, comparative literary study in other parts of the world stresses the politicization of literature and rejects the formalist approach completely. Analysing East–West literary relations, Swapan Majumdar argues that Indian literature, like its African and Latin American counterparts, forms a community of what he calls 'sub-national literatures no less robust than the components of Western literature': 'except for the fact that in the former only literary semblances count for their commonness, while in the latter a common ethos, equally manifest in all, hold them together.'[12] In consequence, he suggests that comparison should take place not across individual cultural boundaries, but on a larger scale altogether:

> Indian Literature . . . should be compared not with any single literature of the West, but with the concept of Western Literature as a whole, while the regional literatures should be assigned the status of constituent sub-national literatures in India.[13]

This proposal derives from a totally different perspective from that of Western comparatists. Majumdar is essentially saying that just as Western scholars chose to use terms such as 'Indian Literature' or 'African Literature' monolithically, thereby disregarding the range of variants of what he calls 'constituent sub-literatures' of those continents, so Indian or African scholars are now opting for such terms as 'Western Literature' or 'European Literature', general classifications that invite re-examination of the old models that placed component literatures of the Western tradition in a position of international superiority.

He also argues that the critical tools borrowed from the West are not necessarily suitable for the study of all literatures, a point made by many African, Asian and Latin American critics too. One immediately obvious question is the problem of periodization, for the relationship between literary tradition and textual production in India or in China, for example, involves a different notion of periodization, indeed a different concept of continuity and history. The fortunes of Indian authors, Majumdar argues, have remained renegotiable across generations because of 'the continuative character of the Indian tradition'. So to accept Western models of literary historiography is to accept a system that forces the Indian tradition into a straight jacket and imposes a European perspective on a non-European vision of the world. Sri Aurobindo draws our attention to the different perspectives and to the dangers of imposing one system upon another, when he discusses the ways in which Indian literature has been devalued by Western critics and offers a hypothetical satirical picture of how Indian readers might have evaluated the great European masterpieces if they had colonized Europe. Such readers would:

> dismiss the *Iliad* as a crude and empty semi-savage and primitive epos, Dante's great work as a nightmare of a cruel and superstitious religious fantasy, Shakespeare as a drunken barbarian of considerable genius with an epileptic imagination, the whole drama of Greece and Spain and England as a mass of bad ethics and violent horrors, French poetry as a succession of bald and tawdry rhetorical exercises and French fiction as a tainted and immoral thing.[14]

Implicit to comparative literature outside Europe and the United States is the need to start with the home culture and to look outwards, rather than to start with the European model of literary excellence and to look inwards. So the founding of the Indian Comparative Literature Association in 1981 stated that the main objective of the new Association was:

> to arrive at a conception of Indian literature which will not only modernize our literature departments but also take care of the task

of discovering the greatness of our literature and to present a panoramic view of Indian literary activities through the ages.

A fundamental task of Indian comparative literature is the assertion of the importance of tradition and the creation of a literary history constructed upon Indian models. Similar views predominate among African comparatists. Chidi Amuta is scathing about the kind of comparative criticism that seeks to trace European influences on African writers and describes 'the quest for influences' as 'one of the ruses in the trick bag' of those critics who see European culture as having had a civilizing impact on 'primitive' African writing.[15] He also complains about the use made by Western comparatists of the term 'universal', citing Chinua Achebe who in 1975 declared that the term was used 'as a synonym for the narrow, self-serving parochialism of Europe'.[16] This discourse is a long way away from the claims made by North American comparatists for the universal civilizing potential of 'Great' works. Comparative literature from this perspective is a political activity, part of the process of reconstructing and reasserting cultural and national identity in the post-colonial period.

Crucial to that process is the question of language. In an essay that looks at the complex process of unnaming and naming for Afro-Americans, Kimberley Benston argues that:

> For the Afro-American, then, self-creation and reformation of a fragmented familial past are endlessly interwoven: naming is inevitably genealogical revisionism. All of Afro-American literature may be seen as one vast genealogical poem that attempts to restore continuity to the ruptures and discontinuities imposed by the history of black presence in America.[17]

The task of renaming is part of the larger task, that of restoring continuity, and we can see the same process taking place all over the world, as comparative literature is being redefined. The role of translation in this process is, of course, crucial, and the conscious decision to translate key European writers such as Shakespeare on the part of Indian or Chinese translators, for example, carries with it a set of assumptions about the status of the target language vis-à-vis the source text. Shakespeare, depicted by nineteenth-century scholars such as Macaulay as the epitome of all things English, the supreme master of the language, is renamed and in consequence reread once he appears in Bengali, Malay or Mandarin. The role of translation in world comparative literature is discussed more fully in chapter 7 below, and it is significant that critical discussion of the problematics of intercultural translation has developed alongside post-colonial theory of the 1970s and 1980s.

Comparative Schools in the 1990s

In the nineteenth century, the principle distinction made in comparative literature was between the French school, with its emphasis on positivism and its attempts to narrow down the criteria for comparing texts, and the German school, with its emphasis on *zeitgeist* and on racial and ethnic roots. The German model was taken over by the Nazis with appalling consequences, as right-wing scholars sought to show that there was literary and historical justification for genocidal policies that ranked the Aryan race as superior to all others. Reaction against this kind of gross simplification of important nineteenth-century thinking about origins and about the significance of oral folk culture resulted in the suppression of an important line of Romantic comparative literature, and it has only quite recently begun to be rehabilitated. In the post-war period the French school dominated comparative studies, until challenged by the American school, with its interdisciplinary approach and its emphasis on the universal values of literature. By the early 1960s there was the positivist model on the one hand and the formalist model on the other. It was not until the early 1970s that these two models came to be seriously challenged, and the alternative models came from outside the Euro-American tradition.

In many parts of the world there are now university departments of Western Literature that presuppose a different categorization from that traditionally adopted by European and European-influenced literature departments. Binary comparative literature sees French and Italian literatures, for example, as differentiated in all kinds of ways – linguistically, geographically, historically, aesthetically. But once both those literatures are included under a general heading of European Literature or Western Literature, it is the similarities and the links between them that come sharply into focus rather than the differences. From the perspective of a student in Japan or in Kenya, for example, what is striking is the common ground between the French and Italian literary traditions, along with the peculiar antagonism noted by Freud when he pointed out that 'Closely related races keep one another at arm's length: the South German cannot endure the North German, the Englishman casts every kind of aspersion upon the Scot, the Spaniard despises the Portuguese.'[18] Viewed from a perspective outside Europe, the parameters change. Moreover, the non-European model of comparative study has as its starting point a very different agenda from that of Western comparative literature. The time has come to recognize that we now have a post-European model of comparative literature, one that reconsiders key questions of cultural identity, literary canons, the political implications of cultural influence, periodization and literary history and firmly rejects the ahistoricity of the American school and of the formalist approach.

In the Introduction, we saw how comparative literature as a subject appears to be declining in the West, even as it is expanding and developing elsewhere in the world. It was argued that literary theory has now become the growth area of literary study in Western Europe and in the United States, probably in reaction against the antiquated methods and complacency of much of the work in comparative literature. But outside the Euro-American tradition those antiquated methods have no place,and instead what we find is a dynamic comparative literature which can effectively be compared to the earliest appearance of the subject in revolutionary Europe in the early nineteenth century. Once divorced from key questions of national culture and identity, comparative literature loses its way. In contexts where the assertion of identity is a central issue, the comparison of literatures and of literary histories, like translation, becomes an important way of reinforcing the cultural starting point. It remains to be seen to what extent the radical changes in former Communist Eastern Europe will lead to new developments in comparative studies along the lines being pursued by emergent and post-colonial nations outside Europe.

The Demise of Classical Education and the Rise of English

While the French school insisted on the importance of linguistic criteria in the process of comparing, and the American school gradually added texts to its list of 'great' works of world literature, comparative literature in Britain occupied a rather curious middle position, shifting uneasily between the two schools.

Where the move towards comparative study came from within Modern Languages departments, the tendency was towards the French school, and where it came from within English departments, the tendency was more towards the American school. However, the Great Books tradition has never been incorporated into the British academic structure, and the continued influence of German Marxist criticism served to weaken the impact of the French positivist approach somewhat. Probably the most original contribution of British comparative literature is the concept of 'placing', the juxtaposing of texts in order to create new readings across cultures. Siegbert Prawer defines placing as:

> the mutual illumination of several texts, or series of texts, considered side by side; the greater understanding we derive from juxtaposing a number of (frequently very different) works, authors and literary traditions.[19]

In similar vein, Henry Gifford suggests that the most useful comparisons:

> are those that writers themselves have accepted or challenged their readers to make – those that spring from the 'shock of recognition' where one writer has become conscious that an affinity exists between another and himself. Henry James felt this about Turgenev, Pound felt it about Propertius, Pushkin about Byron.[20]

Again, we can see this kind of comparative literature as deriving from Matthew Arnold, from the idea that everywhere there is connection, that texts are part of a great intertextual tapestry.

But there is, of course, a great difference between the context in which Matthew Arnold wrote about comparative literature and the context in which Gifford and Prawer wrote about it in the 1970s. Throughout the nineteenth century, passage through the educational system for a Western intellectual meant studying classical languages and having a working acquaintance with other European languages as well. In effect, literary study can be said to have been comparative by definition, since readers had access to texts in different languages. The growth of comparative literature as a subject through the nineteenth century was, paradoxically, parallel to a gradual shift towards monolingualism in Europe and the English-speaking world.

There seem to have been two principle factors in this process. On the one hand, nationalist movements stressed the symbolic significance of national languages, and there were moves in a number of countries to establish Chairs in the national language and literature. On the other hand, throughout the western world, educational systems were moving increasingly towards making clear distinctions between disciplines and subject areas, and towards greater specialization in single, specifically designated subjects. Such a shift was inevitable, given the expansion of industrialization and the need for a new concept of education that sought rather to 'train' people for prospective employment than to 'educate' them according to ideal principles of universal knowledge. The polymath began to give way to the employable specialist. The linguist came increasingly to specialize in a narrow range of languages, often only in one or two.

Of course, the classics continued to be studied until well into the twentieth century, but the study of national literatures began to emerge as a viable alternative. In the English-speaking world, the process took a long time (English did not really become a major university subject until the 1930s), but as Greek and Latin declined dramatically, so modern languages rose to the forefront and specialist departments increased. Whereas a Browning or a Pushkin had read works in various languages without thinking twice about it, a century later the ability to read in several languages was beginning to be considered as a sign of exceptional intelligence and education. Where once knowledge of Greek and Latin was fundamental for any educated European, so by the 1920s that pattern had changed radically and by the 1990s knowledge of Greek and Latin is limited to a small specialist group. Moreover, the status of modern European languages in the nineteenth century is completely altered today. French, once regarded as probably the most important European language, widely used across Central and Eastern Europe and throughout Africa and the Middle East, has fallen into second place behind English, the new world language of commerce and the market-place. This spread of English, combined with the decline of classical languages has also had an impact on comparative literary studies.

In the English-speaking world in particular, it is no longer feasible to insist on linguistic difference as a prerequisite for comparing literatures, because increasingly readers have access to classical languages only in translation and to fewer modern languages as well. The establishment of university departments of French or English or German as independent units, which began promisingly enough, came to mean that comparative study necessarily involved crossing administrative bridges as well as intellectual ones. The French insistence on linguistic competence was often taken up by specialist scholars working from within a given area of study and used as a way of ensuring the continued prestige of their own subject area. So, for example, a number of programmes in comparative literature in the 1960s were set up as a kind of bargain package between language subject areas: French and German, Spanish and Italian, German and Russian, English and any one of the above. This perpetuated the binary distinction, while also ensuring a fairly straightforward administrative structure, involving the collaboration of two departments and no more.

In contrast, those language areas traditionally given less prominence in the Euro-American university system have been taught within what can only be described as a comparative framework. The establishment of Schools or Departments of African Studies, Oriental Studies, Caribbean Studies, Latin American Studies, Arabic Studies, Slavonic Studies, Central Asian Studies, Scandinavian Studies and others may be criticized for enshrining a hierarchical notion of majority and minority cultures (one thinks of European institutions with dozens of specialists in 'major' Western European languages and cultural history, but with only one or two Arabists or Sinologists, for example). But nevertheless, such a structure offers a different set of possibilities for comparative work, since the departmental boundaries, like the single subject boundaries, are not rigidly in place. Moreover, within such entities there are not only literary scholars, but also historians, linguists, economists, sociologists and anthropologists, thereby further extending the range of study that can be undertaken. In other words, although the agglomerative system of putting together the entire African continent under a single heading may derive from a hierarchical notion that prioritizes individual Western European cultures and increasingly lumps everything else together as something 'Other', it nevertheless can be seen in a less negative light when contrasted with the single subject structure. Significantly, the past two decades have seen a steady rise in the status and student numbers of such comparative programmes, further evidence of the movement away from binary study and ahistoricity in literary study.

The spread of English and the decline of classical languages means also that comparative courses increasingly study texts in translation, which leads on to other methodological issues. If texts written in various different languages are read in translation, then one result of this can be reductive, in that they can all be made to appear to be part of the same literary system. A study of the novel of adultery in the nineteenth century, for example, that compares Flaubert's *Madame Bovary*, Tolstoy's *Anna Karenina*, Fontane's *Effie Briest* and George Meredith's *Diana of the Crossways* would be constructed differently according to whether the texts are read in translation or in the original language. Stylistic aspects necessarily fall by the wayside if all the texts are translated, while thematic comparison (thematic in terms of plot and character study) comes to the forefront. This has nothing to do with the quality of a translation; it has everything to do with the way in which readers read, absorbing translated texts into the patterns of familiarity of their own literary system. Inevitably, whether we like it or not, texts come to be seen as 'belonging' to the language into which they are translated; hence Ibsen, Strindberg and Chekov have almost become 'English' playwrights, for their plays are so frequently performed and read and they are so often taught on courses of modern drama in Britain and the United States.

Significantly, until relatively recently, despite the reliance on translation in comparative literature, there has been very little systematic work that examines what happens to a text as it is transferred from one language to another. The rise of translation studies, which parallels the decline of comparative literature, is linked to a number of factors, which will be discussed more fully in chapter 7, but principle among these is the return to a notion of literature that seeks to prioritize cultural difference and not avoid it.

Comparative Literature and Cultural Studies

The 'cultural turn' in translation studies, which happened in the 1980s, was linked to developments in the expanding field of 'cultural studies'. Attempts to define cultural studies have been fraught with pitfalls and conflicts, and the term is about as useful as the term 'comparative literature' was to nineteenth-century scholars facing similar problems, that is, it is more obfuscatory than helpful. However, there are a great many similarities between cultural studies in the 1990s and comparative literature in the last century. Both are interdisciplinary attempts by scholars to cope with a rapidly changing world in which ideas of culture, language, nation, history and identity are in a process of transformation. The nineteenth-century comparatists wrestled with the problems of roots and origins, with determining traditions and establishing a literary canon, with asserting national consciousness and interacting with emergent nation states elsewhere. The more radical scholars posited the greatness of their native literature over the Classical literatures which still ruled supreme.

Likewise, twentieth-century cultural studies scholars struggle with the problem of defining a subject that is essentially a critique of existing disciplines. As Richard Johnson puts it:

> Even now, distinctively 'literary' and distinctively 'sociological' approaches are developing, closely related to theoretical fragmentations. This would not matter if one discipline or one problematic could grasp the study of culture as a whole, but this is not, in my opinion, the case. Cultural processes do not correspond to the contours of academic knowledge as they stand. Cultural studies must be interdisciplinary or a-disciplinary in its tendencies ... we need a special kind of defining activity ... not definition in the sense of an academic codification of cultural studies ... *but some pointers to further transformations.*[21]

Johnson argues that there are three main forms of research in cultural studies: the study of the processes of cultural production, text-based approaches which focus on the cultural products themselves, and research into lived cultures, which 'has been closely associated with a politics of representation'. He also recognizes a debt to feminist theory, which has called into question all kinds of assumptions about literary and cultural history, about categorization systems, about the relationship between the private self and the public sphere of activity. The study of cultural processes, he suggests, is of fundamental importance and yet it defies precise definitions and categories and draws upon a whole range of diverse methodologies. Much the same could be said of the earliest manifestations of comparative literary study, which also defied precise definitions. Unfortunately, successive generations saw fit to try and establish precise definitions regardless, and the history of comparative literature until recently has been the history of that quixotic effort which was doomed to fail from the outset.

Today, comparative literature in one sense is dead. The narrowness of the binary distinction, the unhelpfulness of the ahistorical approach, the complacent shortsightedness of the Literature-as-universal-civilizing-force approach have all contributed to its demise. But it lives on under other guises: in the radical reassessment of Western cultural models at present being undertaken in many parts of the world, in the transcendence of disciplinary boundaries through new methodological insights supplied by gender studies or cultural studies, in the examination of the processes of intercultural transfer that are taking place within translation studies. The remaining chapters of this book consider some of those alternative forms of comparative literary study, and show how the activity of comparison is being both revitalized and politicized in the world today.

3
Comparing the Literatures of the British Isles

Anecdotal Preface

Some years ago, on a visit to the Slovak Academy of Sciences in Bratislava, I was asked by the well-known Slovak comparatist, Dionyz Durisin, to give him the names of colleagues in Britain working on British Comparative Literature. Having been a founder member of the British Comparative Literature Association, and being its treasurer at the time, I felt I had a sound sense of who was working on what, so I duly provided him with a list of names of colleagues in French, German and English departments and the few specifically designated Comparative Literature programmes. He appeared perplexed by this, and repeated his request for names of colleagues working on British Comparative Literature. I assured him the names I had given him were a representative cross section. He pointed out politely that they were all scholars in French, German or English. I repeated that they were our best-known comparatists. We looked at one another across our cups of coffee in bafflement.

It took several minutes before it dawned on me what he was asking me for. He simply wanted to know who was comparing the literatures of the British Isles, for that seemed to him and his colleagues to be the proper business of British comparatists. When I said that there were no such programmes of research or teaching, and that the British Comparative Literature Association had never even considered this question, my statement was met with disbelief. Why not, everyone wanted to know. For which I had no answer.

Following that visit, I began to ask myself why I had found it impossible to answer, and also why there should have been no developments along the lines suggested by Slovak colleagues. The next year I introduced into my Masters programme of Comparative Literary Theory, seminars on the problematics of British comparative literature, which have since grown into an entire course. And in so doing, it has become possible to use the example of the British Isles as a case study of a whole range of problems within comparative literature, problems that the old binary study approach, or any of the formalist approaches, could never hope to tackle, let alone resolve.

Terminological Problems

The first, most immediate problem is terminological. There is a great deal of difference between *Britain*, which is a political entity, and the *British Isles,* which is a geographical one. The *United Kingdom*, a third term, is made up of England, Scotland, Wales and Northern Ireland. The Isle of Man and the Channel Islands are technically not part of the United Kingdom, although they are possessions of the British Crown. The Republic of Ireland or Eire is a separate state, though geographically it can be defined as part of the British Isles. Sorting one's way through the terminology is extremely complex, and it can be deeply offensive to make mistakes. So, for example, if we speak of British comparative literature, to include Irish writers would be an act of appropriation, because Irish work would be subsumed under the heading of British. This has not stopped generations of scholars from doing just that (how many English literature syllabuses feature Yeats and Joyce, for example?), though Weisstein considers any attempt to distinguish between English and Irish literatures as 'misguided methodological purism' (see pp. 29 and 37 above). Seamus Heaney has a very different view. In his famous 'Open Letter' (1983) written in protest against his inclusion in the 1982 *Penguin Book of Contemporary British Poetry*, edited by Blake Morrison and Andrew Motion, he states unequivocally:

> I hate to bite
> Hands that led me to the limelight
> In the Penguin book, I regret
> The awkwardness.
> But British, no, the name's not right.[1]

The name is not right unless there is a *de facto* assumption that *Britain* as a term can apply to states not subject to the British Crown, which would be unacceptable. This is not misguided methodological purism, it is a fundamental question of principle. A way out of the difficulty, for comparative purposes then, is to abandon the term *British*, and to propose instead a comparative study of the literatures of the British Isles.

Languages, Dialects and Identity

In his book *The Languages of Britain*, Glanville Price specifically excludes the Irish of the Republic of Ireland, for he recognizes the implications of the term Britain.[2] His study is an historical one, but we can borrow his categories and adapt them to the twentieth century, in which case the linguistic map of the British Isles would consist principally of Celtic languages (Erse, Irish of Northern Ireland, Scots Gaelic, and Welsh, as living languages, with a body of texts in Manx and Cornish) and Germanic languages (English, Scots and Norse), with Channel Island French and a growing number of languages in daily use within immigrant communities. The problem for a comparatist is that knowledge of the Celtic and Germanic languages is unevenly distributed. English dominates, and the marginalization of Celtic languages has meant that they tend to be learned *in situ* only. Schools in England may teach French or German; they do not teach the Celtic languages of the British Isles, which are seen as belonging to ethnic groups. What this means is that there are some scholars practising a form of comparative study of Celtic languages, but only from within a framework of Celtic Studies, or Irish Studies or Scottish Studies.

The Scottish question is made more complex by the rise in the twentieth century of Scots or Lallans, a Germanic language and a variant of English. Glanville Price claims that he changed his mind four times before deciding to consider Scots a language and not simply a dialect of English.[3] He notes, as others have done, that if the distinction between language and dialect were made on linguistic criteria alone, then Danish, Swedish and Norwegian would scarcely be classified as separate languages. That they are classified as languages has everything to do with political power, with the fact that each of those Scandinavian variants is the language of a different nation state. The Scottish question is therefore an especially delicate one, since Scotland is technically part of the United Kingdom, though it can be argued that there has been a flourishing literature in Scots going back well into the fourteenth century.

If we apply the criteria for comparison established by the followers of the binary study tradition, that is, that comparison must take place across linguistic boundaries, we find ourselves in a ludicrous position with the literatures of the British Isles. Following this to its limits, it would mean that only a bilingual scholar who had a Celtic language and English, could undertake comparative study, and it would also mean that Scots, Anglo-Welsh and Anglo-Irish would be excluded because the boundary between their status as languages and as dialects would be unclear. The result would be an affirmation of the hegemony of English, with further marginalization of the literary production of Wales, Scotland and Northern Ireland.

The problem of dialect also applies to English English. Henry Wyld, in the early twentieth century, defined Standard English as a class dialect, arguing that this form of English is common to educated classes regardless of regional origin:

> If we can truthfully say of a man that he has a Scotch [sic] accent, or a Liverpool accent, or a London accent, or a Gloucestershire accent, then he does not speak 'good English' with perfect purity.[4]

A few years later, in his *English for the English*, George Sampson returned to the question of defining Standard English and declared that:

> we know what is *not* standard English, and that is a sufficiently practical guide. If any one wants a definite example of standard English we can tell him that it is the kind of English spoken by a simple unaffected young Englishman like the Prince of Wales.[5]

Standard English, then, was and is a class dialect, untainted by regional accent and the model speaker the future King of England. Hardly surprising to note the strong feelings against the English language held by inhabitants of Wales, Scotland or Ireland. The writer Saunders Lewis, one of the founders of the Welsh Nationalist Party, complained that

Neither language nor dialect have we, we do not know an insult,
And our master gift to history is the MPs we send to Parliament.[6]

while Hugh MacDiarmid, the great poet of the Scots revival,
declared:

> I stand still for forces which
> were subjugated to mak' way
> for England's poo'er, and to enrich
> The kinds o' English, and o' Scots,
> The least congenial to my thoughts.[7]

What these writers are doing is to reflect in verse the sentiments
expressed over a century earlier by the Irish writer and founder of
The Nation, Thomas Davis (1814–45), in an essay on language and
national identity, when he wrote: 'How unnatural – how corrupting
'tis for us, three-fourths of whom are of Celtic blood, to speak a
medley of Teutonic dialects . . . What business have we with the
Norman-Sassenagh?'[8] Davis, like so many subsequent Irish, Welsh
and Scottish writers, was all too aware of the intrinsic links between
language and national consciousness and identity. The suppression
of Celtic languages, the penalization of Celtic speakers, the process
of Anglicizing place names and baptismal names that went on for
centuries left a legacy of bitterness as strong as that felt today by
ethnic groups along the Baltic or in Central Asia obliged to use
Russian in accordance with the policy of the former Soviet Union.
It also politicized writers, and John Williams, though he uses the
adjective 'British' in ways that remain very contentious, sums up the
current situation rather neatly:

> It has fallen to the lot of Scottish, Irish and Welsh poets to provide
> the most insistent note of political awareness within the main-
> stream of British poetry . . . England is viewed tangentially by the
> rest of Britain, whose economic and social problems may be seen as
> visited upon them. For Scotland, Wales and Ireland there exist
> alternative cultural and linguistic perspectives, and often a more
> natural sense of relationships both with Europe and the United
> States.[9]

The editors of the Penguin anthology that Seamus Heaney objected
to for the all-inclusive use of the word 'British' talk about some

writers having 'lived in important places', a slightly curious way of describing the feelings of marginality and of resistance to the centrality of England and English over the centuries that has so often been articulated in literary texts. And it is Heaney who presents the counter view to the very English perspective of Blake Morrison and Andrew Motion, when he writes:

> Caesar's Britain, its *partes tres*,
>   United England, Scotland, Wales,
> *Britannia* in the old tales,
>   Is common ground.
> *Hibernia* is where the Gaels
>   Made a last stand.
>
> And long ago were stood upon-
> End of simple history lesson.
> As empire rings its curtain down
>   This 'British' word
> Sticks deep in native and *colon*
>   Like Arthur's sword.[10]

Heaney's 'Open Letter' draws our attention to the importance of history in understanding the present, and this is one of the most significant differences between writers from across the British Isles. The Northern Irish poet John Hewitt's poem, 'An Irishman in Coventry', refers to 'eight hundred years disaster',[11] meaning the history of English domination of Ireland. The persistence of history in the literatures of Ireland, Scotland and Wales, history understood in a special way as an account of an ongoing struggle for national identity, is in marked contrast to the English version of history, which traces instead the gradual rise to world dominance of the English language and its literature.

The Significance of History

Any attempt at comparing the literatures of the British Isles must have an historical dimension. The linguistic and cultural diversities within the British Isles need to be set in context, and it is not enough to work with the boundaries that can be drawn at the present time, be they linguistic, geographical or political.

The present political division dates from the founding of the Irish Free State in 1922, which became the Republic of Ireland in 1937. Scotland was joined to England through the accession of the Scottish King, James Stuart, in 1603, following the death of the childless English Queen, Elizabeth I, and any hopes of a Stuart restoration ended when the Hanoverians crushed the second Jacobite Rising in 1745. Wales had been incorporated in the thirteenth century, and although a guerrilla war was fought for several centuries, the accession of the Tudors signalled the absorption of Wales into what would eventually become the United Kingdom in 1536.

But the political map does not correspond to a linguistic map, nor to the pattern of widely different literary traditions. The nine-teenth century, the age of nationalist movements across Europe, had repercussions in the British context as well, with a revival of interest in Celtic languages in general. The last native Cornish speaker, for example, died in the eighteenth century, but Cornish was being revived as a literary language by the end of the nineteenth century, and work has continued on the reconstruction of this dead Celtic language to the present day, despite the fact that Cornwall is technically a region of England and has no autonomy whatsoever. The Isle of Man, on the other hand, has never been absorbed administratively into the United Kingdom and is self-governed to a large degree, being unrepresented in the House of Commons. Its language, Manx, died out as a spoken tongue in the 1950s and 60s, which means that there are still extant tapes of native speakers, as well as a body of written texts.

Both Cornish and Manx are Celtic languages, but have virtually disappeared. In contrast, Irish, Welsh and Scots Gaelic have been undergoing a living revival, for reasons that have everything to do with a reassertion of national identity through the medium of language. So when invited to contribute to an anthology of con-temporary Scottish poetry, Sorley Maclean, the great Scots Gaelic poet of the twentieth century, chose his poem 'The National Museum of Ireland' (1970):

> because it too has so much of history in it, so much of the tragic history of Scotland and of the world as well as of Ireland. A Gael, if he is at all a Gael, must love Ireland as well as Scotland.[12]

There is no space here even to attempt a proper discussion of the revival of Celtic languages over the past century, but the important point to note is that such a revival has been taking place, and that despite the dominance of English there are a great many speakers of Welsh, Irish and Gaelic, and a flourishing literary and performance tradition in all three. It is also important to note that the production of texts in the Celtic languages derives not only from the need to assert the aesthetic values of the language, but also from an oppositional position. Any comparison of texts that fails to note this fundamental issue would not get very far.

It is, of course, far too simplistic to suggest that national identity is necessarily linked to the surviving practice of text creation in the Celtic languages, and the numbers of powerful writers in Ireland, Scotland, Wales and England all testify to the way in which English, the hegemonic language, can be used in diverse ways. But it is important to note the need for continuity with the past that emerges in the work of Anglophone British writers equally with Celtic ones. Michael O'Loughlin, a product of the twentieth-century mass media world, rejects and then immediately reassesses his relationship to the mythical Irish hero, Cuchulainn, in his poem of the same name:

> If I lived in this place for a thousand years
> I could never construe you, Cuchulainn.
> Your name is a fossil, a petrified tree
> Your name means less than nothing[. . .]
> But watching TV the other night
> I began to construe you Cuchulainn:
> You came on like some corny revenant
> In a black-and-white made for TV
> American Sci-fi serial.[13]

Here, then, is an English-speaking Irish writer looking back at his Celtic mythic inheritance. The importance of the world of Celtic myth for contemporary writers is enormous, for it offers an alternative to the Teutonic mythology of the Anglo-Saxon world. John Montague, the Northern Irish poet, sums up this sense of being in touch with an ancestral past in the last lines of his poem 'Like Dolmens Round My Childhood, the Old People':

> Ancient Ireland, indeed! I was reared by her bedside,
> The rune and the chant, evil eye and averted head,
> Fomorian fierceness of family and local feud.
> Gaunt figures of fear and friendliness,

For years they trespassed on my dreams,
Until once, in a standing circle of stones,
I felt their shadows pass
Into that dark permanence of ancient forms.[14]

The past recalled by those writers who, like Norman MacCaig, see themselves as 'being helplessly / lugged backwards / through the debatable lands of history'[15] is not the same past as that proclaimed from Westminster. Nor is it the same past as the one traditionally taught under the guise of history of English literature. *The Pelican Guide to English Literature*, that trusted stalwart used by students since the 1950s and divided into seven separate volumes brings Irish and Scottish writers under the definition of English literature without a qualm. In volume I, *The Age of Chaucer*, John Speirs' chapter 'A Survey of Medieval Verse' states baldly that 'The most living poetry in the fifteenth century and early sixteenth century until we come to Wyatt was composed in Scotland, for it is unlikely that even the Skelton enthusiasts would claim that he is the equal of the Scots poet Dunbar.'[16] But despite such praise, Scots writing is firmly included within the boundaries of English literature in this and subsequent volumes.

It is, of course, a fact that English literature enjoys a particularly exalted place in the world, partly through the influence of individual writers and more recently through the prominence of the English language. But we are on uncertain ground when we try to apply that prominent position retrospectively. Let us, for argument's sake, consider comparatively the literary production of the British Isles at a series of moments in the past, and ascertain the point at which English began to move into the forefront ahead of other literatures from the same geographical area.

The Norman conquest of 1066 ended the role of the Saxons and Danes in England, and the impact of that invasion has tended to obscure other patterns of territorial change that were taking place elsewhere. The great programmes of castle and cathedral building, and the spread of monasteries through former Saxon territories is a familiar story. Less familiar, however, are the gradual decline into anarchy in England and the power of the Norwegians in the northern parts of the British Isles. Just two years before the death in 1100 of William II – son of Duke William, who became the first of the Norman kings of England – Magnus of Norway had seized the

Orkneys, the Hebrides and the Isle of Man. In 1103 he invaded Ireland, and it is likely that the constant struggles against the Norse invaders weakened the country and left it open to conquest by the Normans in 1169.

During the reign of Stephen (1135–54) William of Malmesbury wrote: 'England is become the dwelling place of foreigners and the property of strangers. At the present time there is no Englishman who is either earl, bishop or abbot. Strangers prey upon the riches and vitals of England, nor is there any hope of an end to this misery.[17] War, invasion, appropriation of land, the destruction of the old order, radical changes to language, all the miseries accompanying colonization characterize the situation in England in the early twelfth century. And with the passing of the old order, there came also radical changes to literary models. Almost a century was to pass from the time of William of Malmesbury's complaint to the appearance of Lazamon's alliterative poem the *Brut*, which marks a new stage of development of English verse.

If we compare the state of literary production and of libraries across the British Isles around the time of the Norman conquest, we find a flourishing oral poetry in Wales and Ireland, in contrast to the Saxon tradition which had sunk into decline. Indeed, the great Arthurian cycles which were to spread across Europe came out of the Welsh and Breton tradition. The Irish libraries had been one of the glories of Europe for centuries. During the so-called Dark Ages, scholars and members of the nobility flocked to Ireland to take advantage of the Irish schools, and the Venerable Bede notes that Anglo-Saxons studying in Ireland in the seventh century were given gratuitous instruction. So advanced was the state of learning in Irish institutions that it has been suggested that the European Renaissance was anticipated by several centuries:

> The classic tradition to all appearances dead in Europe, burst into full flower in the Isle of Saints, and the Renaissance began in Ireland 700 years before it was known in Italy. During three centuries Ireland was the asylum of the higher learning which took sanctuary there from the uncultured states of Europe. At one time Armagh, the religious capital of Christian Ireland, was the metropolis of civilization.[18]

Alongside the Christian tradition, of course, there was a vastly rich mythology, preserved within the Bardic tradition, as was also the case in Wales. In the mid-twelfth century the great *Book of Leinster* was compiled, a vast collection of ancient Irish legends. But the Anglo-Norman invasion effectively choked the cultural life of Ireland, the great centres of learning decayed and there began a long period of permanent war which, as Douglas Hyde puts it 'almost from its very commencement *thoroughly arrested Irish develop-ment, and disintegrated Irish life*'.[19]

Four centuries later, the comparative picture of literary pro-duction changes completely. Though the Renaissance flowered in continental Europe, its arrival in England was delayed, due to the effects of a long period of civil war. In Ireland, the bardic tradition dominated, but the colonial wars had taken their toll, and successive rulers had endeavoured to suppress what was seen as a subversive activity. In the sixteenth century the Act of Elizabeth declared:

> for that those rhymours by their ditties and rhymes made to divers lords and gentlemen in Ireland to the commendation and high praise of extortion, rebellion, rape, ravin and other injustice, encourage those lords and gentlemen rather to follow those vices than to leave them, and for making of the said rhymes rewards are given by the said lords and gentlemen, [let] for abolishing of so heinous abuse, orders be taken.[20]

The penalty for subversive rhyming was death.

In Scotland, however, the Renaissance came parallel with devel-opments in the rest of Europe, and the second half of the fifteenth century is one of the greatest periods of literary richness in Scottish history. Among the great figures of the age are the young King James I (1394–1437), Robert Henryson (c.1425–1505), William Dunbar (c.1460–c.1520), Gavin Douglas (c.1475–1522) and Sir David Lindsay (1490–1555). There was also a great deal of translation in Scots, and the wealth of poetry produced in the so-called Golden Age of Scots Literature stands in sharp contrast to the paucity of works produced in England at the same time. Moreover, the gap between the two nations was perceived as unbridgeably wide. *The Complaynt of Scotland*, printed in 1549, states baldly that:

> There is nocht twa nations under the firmament that ar mair contrar and different fra uthers nor is inglis men and scottis men, quhoubeit that thei be vitht in ane ile and nychtbours, and of ane langage.[21]

The author of *The Complaynt* also had linguistic politics on his agenda:

> I thocht it nocht necessair til hef fardit ande lardit this tracteit witht exquisite termis, quhilkis are nocht daily usit, bot rather I hef usit domestic Scottis langage, maist intelligibil for the vulgare pepil.[22]

Full political union between England and Wales took place in 1536, when Welsh law was abolished and the Parliament in London became responsible also for Wales. The bardic tradition was in decline, and full political union accelerated its demise. However, as Thomas Parry has argued in his ground-breaking history of Welsh literature, the combination of political union and the Protestant Reformation brought about a leap forward in Welsh prose writing. That leap forward happened, as it so often does, in times of cultural transition, through translation.

In the latter part of the sixteenth century, the Bible was translated into Welsh. Parry sees this translation as the salvation of Welsh literary language:

> When the gentry should have become finally anglicized, and the strict poets have fallen silent, there would be nobody left who knew the pure Welsh which was once the common heritage of the whole country. The Bible came, and it came just in time, when the dignified tongue was still alive, and when there were Welsh priests sufficiently master of it to be able to use it appropriately.[23]

The Bible, Parry feels, gave Wales standard Welsh, a literary language which, in a country 'which lacked a university or any cultural institution', was to serve as a focal point.

The Renaissance in England, arriving later than in Scotland, coincided with the start of the age of discovery, the beginning of English colonial expansion. From the seventeenth century onwards, through the English Revolution and the Restoration, large numbers of texts were translated voraciously into English and large numbers of sailing vessels carried slaves across the Atlantic, settlers to the colonies and goods back into English ports. Guerrilla warfare, exacerbated by religious conflict, continued with considerable savagery in Ireland and in Scotland. By the end of the eighteenth century, the start of the Age of Romanticism, another period of great literary development in English, the picture across the British Isles had again changed completely.

The savage reprisals following the abortive Stuart rebellion of 1745 and the subsequent policy of depopulation of the Scottish Highlands had driven Gaelic into the wilderness. In both Scotland and Ireland the wretched poverty of the mainly rural population led millions to emigrate in search of a better life. Moreover, the changing class structure had created an English-speaking gentry in both countries, with the Celtic languages despised and outlawed. The singer and composer Michael Kelly recounts how he had an audience with the Emperor of Germany at Schoenbrunn, in the presence of some Irish officers, one of whom spoke to him in Irish. Unable to answer, Kelly stayed silent:

> The Emperor turned quickly on me and said, 'What! O'Kelly, don't you speak the language of your own country?' I replied, 'Please, your Majesty, none but the lower orders of the Irish people speak Irish'. The Emperor laughed loudly. The impropriety of the remark made before two Milesian Generals flashed into my mind in an instant, and I could have bitten off my tongue. They luckily did not, or pretended not to hear.[24]

Despite the attempts to suppress Scots Gaelic and Irish, both languages, like Welsh, survived. Through the nineteenth century, inspired by the revolutionary ideas in circulation throughout Europe following the French Revolution, their significance increased. But by the end of the eighteenth century the cultural interface between Dublin, Edinburgh and London had gone beyond any sense of binary opposition between Celtic and Teutonic linguistic systems. While the peasantry starved in the Gaelic-speaking rural hinterland, it had become possible to discern a new Anglo-Irish intelligentsia and in Scotland, as Nicholas Phillipson puts it, in his book on the Enlightenment in national context:

> By the 1760s Scotland had become a centre of learning and letters of international importance ... Scottish learning meant the histories of David Hume and William Robertson, the poems of Ossian, the philosophical novels of Tobias Smollett and Henry Mackenzie, the moral literary and philosophical essays of Hume and Mackenzie's *Mirror* and *Lounger*. By the early nineteenth century that history would also have included Robert Burns and Sir

Walter Scott and the literary and political journalism of Francis Jeffrey's *Edinburgh Review*. In the university classrooms of Germany, France and America, Scottish learning meant the philosophical treatises of Adam Smith, Alan Ferguson, Thomas Reid, James Beattie and Dugald Stewart, the aesthetic writings of Lord Kames and Hugh Blair and the medical textbooks of Edinburgh university.[25]

To which we might also add the ground-breaking work of Alexander Fraser Tytler, published in 1791, the first theoretical study of the principles of translation.

What can we deduce from this quick skimming across the centuries? Firstly, that the predominance of English and of English literature is a relatively recent phenomenon, and coincides with the rise of the mercantile classes in the late seventeenth and eighteenth centuries, and with increased colonial expansion overseas. Secondly, that English expansion into the Celtic cultures of the British Isles has been characterized by a conscious strategy of linguistic discrimination, that sought to suppress those languages that were seen as cultural signifiers of resistance and hostility to English rule. Thirdly, that it is hardly surprising, given such circumstances, that the revival of nationalism which swept Europe in the nineteenth century, fuelled by the twin successes of the American Revolution and then the French Revolution, should have had its impact on Welsh, Scottish and Irish writers and intellectuals, and should have led to a revival of interest in Celtic languages and the Celtic tradition.

But it must also be remembered that unlike the Czech revival, for example, there was no consensus on the need to use the 'national' language, for the suppression of Celtic languages had resulted in a peasantry who operated in spoken Welsh, Gaelic or Irish and a class of intellectuals who operated in their own variant of English. This meant that although the folklore movement of the nineteenth century consciously sought out native speakers as continuers of the ancient bardic tradition, most Irish or Scottish philosophers, historians, novelists and political scientists wrote and published in English.

As Sean Lucy, editor of a volume of Irish poets in English says, attempting to define Anglo-Irish poetry, there is still 'on the one hand a complex and developing relationship between two traditions, two cultures, two languages, and on the other, it is the story of a search; it is part of the quest of the English-speaking Irish for an identity, the reshaping of English to express the Irish experience.'[26] In considering the British Isles at any point in time it is not enough to draw up maps that show variations in language distribution. Other factors need considering too, such as the relationship between urban and rural communities, changes in the educational system and the impact of such changes on class patterns, and the huge variations in religious beliefs and practices that have been and continue to be so crucial. It is completely inadequate to conceive of any of the component states of the British Isles in an undifferentiated socio-cultural continuum, and it is noteworthy that so much critical thinking has indeed pursued such a line, similar to the kind of globalized generalizations about 'African' or 'Latin American' literature which will be discussed in the next chapter.

The failure of comparative literature scholars within the British Isles to consider comparatively the development of different literary traditions within their proper historical context remains an unhappy reminder of the formalist legacy in a subject that has tried to present itself as innovative and transcultural. A great deal of rethinking has been going on in the Celtic diaspora, and the steady rise of Scottish Studies and of Irish Studies as international disciplines through the 1980s testifies to that process. The relationship of the Celtic diaspora to the English mainstream still remains to be properly investigated, and as Sean Richards puts it: 'The relationship of England and Ireland, colonizer and colonized, within a small western European archipelago has to be re-thought and re-read, and art and culture on all dimensions and levels of complexity must seek to provide the single-word spark to an inextinguishable thought.'[27]

Parochial and Provincial

According to Siegbert Prawer, the most ambitious type of comparative literary study 'is that which undertakes to define and compare different national traditions'[28] This is probably correct, if what is attempted is a definition of national traditions, because inevitably the comparatist would fall into generalization based on culturally constructed stereotypes. Prawer examines some of the early attempts to define national characteristics, to establish the 'spirit' of a nation as reflected in language and literature, and what emerges from his discussion is the lack of any coherent theory of cultural transfer. This lack, which is a characteristic of a great deal of comparative literature, becomes particularly acute when, as we can see, the political, economic and social questions involving the transfer of texts (or lack of it) from one culture to another are fundamental, as is the case with any attempt to compare the literatures of the British Isles. We have to confront the hegemony of English before comparison can take place, and once that confrontation starts, all kinds of questions relating to minority/majority cultures come out into the open. The questions posed by Pierre Bourdieu, in his 'Le paradoxe du sociologue', are applicable here, for there are certainly several different categorizing systems operating as we move from culture to culture:

> one of the fundamental problems which the theory of the perception of the social world poses is the problem of the relationship between learned and common knowledge. The act of construction – is it the act of the learned or the indigenous? Has the indigenous some categories of perception and from where does he gain them, and what is the relationship between the categories constructed by science and the categories which ordinary agents put into practice?[29]

Patrick Kavanagh (1904–67), the great Irish poet, discusses the use writers make of national myths, and the gap between ordinary lived experience and the construct of a myth of a nation. 'Is Synge the voice of Ireland?' he asks; '*Has* Ireland a voice?'[30] And in questioning the meaning of the national myth, he expounds his theory of parochialism and provincialism, a crucial distinction that offers an alternative way of perceiving the literary output of the British Isles:

> Parochialism and provincialism are opposites. The provincial has no mind of his own; he does not trust what his eyes see until he has heard what the metropolis – towards which his eyes are turned – has to say on any subject. This runs through all activities.
> The parochial mentality, on the other hand, is never in any doubt about the social and artistic validity of his parish . . . In Ireland we are inclined to be provincial not parochial, for it requires a great deal of courage to be parochial. When we do attempt having

the courage of our parish we are inclined to go false and play up to the larger parish on the other side of the Irish Sea. In recent times we have had two great Irish parishioners – James Joyce and George Moore. They explained nothing. The public had either to come to them or stay in the dark . . .

Parochialism is universal; it deals with the fundamentals.[31]

Kavanagh's distinction between parochial and provincial is an important one. In the context in which he used the term, he was reproaching fellow Irish writers for their provincialism, another way of describing the double bind of either following the main-stream (i.e. English) models or reacting against them. But he also touches upon the hierarchical relationship between the secondary margins and the primary centre, and in proposing the universality of parochialism, he effectively deconstructs that hierarchy.

By focusing not on the general but on the specific, by establishing a set of criteria, be they aesthetic or social, that are determined parochially, the writer can draw readers into his or her world. So Jackie Kay, the black Scottish poet, for example, in her 1991 collection comprising *The Adoption Papers and Severe Gale 8* creates the parochial world of a northern adolescent girl of the 1990s, caught between a conflicting set of social expectations and conventions, and draws us willy nilly into that world:

> I don't talk of this. Even memories
> lead to trouble. Especially memories.
> Which school. What house. Which friend.
> We were brought up on different worlds:
> she on mince and potatoes, drizzle, midges;
> me on mealies, thunderstorms, chjongoladas.[32]

Jackie Kay's dramatic poetry portrays characters in a contemporary urban context. Hugh MacDiarmid expresses the parochial/provin-cial distinction in terms of insider/outsider perceptions of the natural environment when he writes:

> Scotland small? Our multiform, our infinite Scotland *small*?
> Only as a patch of hillside may be a cliché corner
> To a fool who cries 'Nothing but heather!' where in Sepember
>   another
> Sitting there and resting and gazing round

Sees not only the heather but blaeberries
With bright green leaves and leaves already turned scarlet,
Hiding ripe blue berries; and amongst the sage-green leaves
Of the bog-myrtle the golden flowers of the tormentil shining[33]

Both writers, however, in their very different ways, are representative of Scottish parochialism, for both write about what Kavanagh called *the fundamentals* in their different ways. And indeed, if we look at a range of poets writing in the British Isles at the present time, that parochial/provincial distinction would provide a good point of comparison. Geoffrey Hill, for example, using his native Black Country as a starting point, or Tony Harrison, Northern poet and translator, are two English poets who would stand comparison with Scottish or Irish writers in these terms, and it may well be that such a comparison would be more fruitful than one based on 'national' distinctions.

Comparative Britains

We began by arguing that literature produced by writers of the British Isles could not be compared without an understanding of the problematics of 'Britishness', and that the difficulties of using the term 'British' could not be understood without some sense of the use made of that term at different moments in the past. The dominance of English as a language, as a literature and as a political system has resulted in a marginalization of a great deal of marvelous writing from elsewhere in the islands.

So powerful has England become, that many students learning English see Britain as a synonym for England, and some even see London as synonymous with England. The terminology of 'English literature' or 'English Studies' is used all-embracingly, so that Welsh, Scottish, Northern Irish and Irish writers are frequently included within a syllabus without any reference to their different point of origin and different literary traditions. This tendency must surely have contributed in large part to the absence of attempts to create a comparative literature of the British Isles, combined with the difficulties presented by the underlying political agenda. Kavanagh may claim Joyce as a truly parochial Irish writer, but a great many English literature courses have taken Joyce over and placed him alongside D. H. Lawrence and Virginia Woolf as an example of English modernism. Acknowledging the existence of Irish literature would impoverish a great many English Literature degrees.

Today, with the benefit of post-colonial theory as it is developing, with the methodological tools provided by gender-based criticism (and a cultural studies expert like Richard Johnson or a Marxist critic like Terry Eagleton both acknowledge their debt to feminist work, in returning the personal to the forefront and abolishing the myth of objectivity in literary scholarship), it is becoming possible to think of comparing the literatures of the British Isles without resorting to discriminatory or appropriatory tactics. Contemporary poetry offers an especially rich field, and considerations of the different ways of representing shared experience of the urban-rural divide, of the significance of place both literally, historically and mythically, and of the relationships between the individual and his or her environment would all be well worth exploring on a comparative basis. The persistence of elegiac poetry, for example, which is common to a great many writers from different parts of the British Isles, could provide an opportunity to explore the contrasts and similarities in form, style and content. So, for example, we could consider Alun Llewellyn-Williams' 1940 'Here in the Quiet fields', which offers a Welshman's perspective on the encroaching war:

> No use to be angry at this interference,
> At the rush of the engines of war;
> Society, gone rotten, is ending, is ending,
> To the tune of the grief and the pain and the last sighing[34]

in comparison with Paul Durcan's 'Ireland, 1972':

> Next to the fresh grave of my beloved grandmother
> The grave of my first love murdered by my brother.[35]

or Ian Crichton-Smith's 1959 'Seagulls':

> . . . at the centre is
> the single-headed seagull in the blue
> image you make for it, its avarice
> its only passion that is really true.
> You cannot admire it even. It is simply
> a force that, like a bomb slim as a death,
> plunges, itself, no other, through the ample
> imperial images that disguise your truth.[36]

and Geoffrey Hill's 'Idylls of the King' (1978):

> 'O clap your hands' so that the dove takes flight,
> bursts through the leaves with an untidy sound,
> plunges its wings into the green twilight
>
> above this long-sought and forsaken ground,
> the half-built ruins of the new estate,
> warheads of mushrooms round the filter-pond[37]

Anthony Thorlby, one of the great British comparatists who looked across to Europe for the objects of his comparative work, stated that literature has an immediacy that engages the reader with 'other things than beauty': 'It is the variety of this experience on subjects like fear and freedom and forgiveness which may in the end form the basis of comparative studies, in conjunction with non-literary materials bearing on the same questions.'[38] Thorlby posits here an approach that could well be applicable as a model for a comparative literature of the British Isles. For it is precisely the variety of experience that writers use as their source material that exposes the fallacy of assuming that merely because English is the hegemonic language and London the seat of the British government, English writing should necessarily be seen as the dominant centre. Indeed, the impact of non-English writers whose native language is a variant of English is leading gradually to a shift in terminology: we now distinguish between 'English Literature' and 'Literature in English', a shift that has happened in the last two decades but which is crucially important for the future. Praising the new impulse given to English, C. D. Narasimhaiah argues:

> that it is not the language of any region is precisely its strength, and its extraordinary cosmopolitan character – its Celtic imaginativeness, the Scottish vigor, the Saxon concreteness, the Welsh music and the American brazenness – suits the intellectual temper of modern India and a composite culture like ours. English is not a pure language but a fascinating combination of tongues welded into a fresh unity.[39]

In the introduction to their collection of essays on comparative literature in the late 1980s, Clayton Koelb and Susan Noakes discuss the changes that have taken place in comparative studies over the past two decades. They point out that interest in the study of movements and literary periods has waned, as has genre study and history of criticism. They note the rising interest in what they describe as 'minor' genres such as biography and the 'intersection (or lack of it) between generic categories in Western and Eastern criticism'.[40] New areas represented in their book include women's studies, the history of education, semiotics and theory of reading. They summarize these trends as follows:

> One can discern a tendency to move away from matters that have been considered essential to the understanding of the history of literature as a great and unified cultural enterprise (movements, themes, periods, the history of ideas) and toward issues that range round the frontier ('emergent' literatures, relationship to other disciplines, women's studies, marginalized forms of reading: 'Pre-reading', 'female-reading', and 'lethetic reading'). This general movement away from the traditional centre of critical discourse is, of course, a feature of much of today's literary scholarship and is not in any way special to Comparative Literature.[41]

Koelb and Noakes suggest that the changes in comparative literature which their book seeks to demonstrate reflect wider changes in literary scholarship. This is undoubtedly true, but it is also the case that by even beginning to consider such questions as the definition of culture, the construction of Otherness, the horizon of reader expectation, the processes of textual transfer through translation, the relationship of language and place, and language and identity, comparative literary study is forced to move away from formalism and into much more risky, but more exciting and dynamic areas of comparative cultural research. The British Isles offers an ideal starting point for an exploration of these new approaches.

Let us conclude this discussion with Seamus Heaney again. 'An Open Letter'was written, as has already been noted, as an occasional piece, in reaction against what the poet saw as improper use of the term 'British' with regard to himself. The poem consists of thirty-three stanzas, and offers a wittily argued case. Stanza ten offers different perspectives on the commonality or difference of history proposed by writers, and stanza eleven appears to go along with the universal approach, in which they are all part of 'a new common-wealth of art' . But the ironic use of mock-poetic language and the contrast between the words 'commonwealth' and 'independent' in

adjacent lines point to the speaker's real position. In stanza thirteen
he calls upon Livy and Horace as examples to follow, and by stanza
sixteen is proclaiming:

> You'll understand I draw the line
> At being robbed of what is mine,
> My *patria* . . .

Heaney's poem is a tour de force, because it presents a deeply
personal view of the Northern Irish writer's predicament, and does
it by constructing a comparative case. The tragic history of Ireland
combines with references to troubled Roman poets, the myth of
Mother Ireland combines with classical mythology, with images of
rape (Philomel and Leda); an imaginary portrait of Ireland contrasts
with a depiction of the London literary world; the English perspective, as exemplified by Donald Davie, who is the object of quite
savage scorn, is contrasted with the brutal reality of divided families
and civil strife. The poem concludes with a twentieth-century fable
set in a cinema, as narrated by the dissident Czech writer Miroslav
Holub, and so Heaney pulls together different threads: his own
dissidence is set in context, compared with Holub's dissidence, and
both writers are presented as continuers of an ancient tradition.

'An Open Letter' is a poem that could not have been written
without a wide range of knowledge of the literatures of other
cultures on the one hand, and a deeply rooted sense of personal
identity in a specific context on the other. It is in effect an exemplary
piece of comparative literature, for in the process of reading it
we are invited to follow Heaney's thought processes, backwards in
time, across cultural boundaries, questioning and challenging
assumptions, insisting ultimately on the need for the process of
naming to be shared. 'British no,' he says simply, 'the name's not
right', following that penultimate line with his own signature:
'Yours truly, Seamus'.

Like Heaney's poem, comparative literary study of the British
Isles has to begin and end with a rethinking of the processes of
naming. In this respect such an enterprise is closely linked to similar
processes of naming and re-naming that are underway in other post-
colonial contexts, as will be seen in the next chapter.

4

Comparative Identities in the Post-Colonial World

In 1492, as the old children's rhyme goes, Columbus sailed the ocean blue. Landing in the Bahamas at first, he then sailed along the coast of Cuba and Hispaniola before returning to Spain to announce that he had discovered an alternative route to the Orient. His *Journal* refers to the Great Khan (*el Gran Can*) that he imagined must live somewhere in the interior of the lands whose coastline he was following, for the main purpose of the voyage was to establish an alternative route to Asia. So strong was the belief that by crossing the Atlantic ships could reach Cathay or India that, despite evidence to the contrary which continued to accumulate, the terminology of the voyagers prolonged the myth. The use of the term 'Indian' to refer to an inhabitant of the Americas was recorded in English in 1618, while the first use of the same adjective to refer to someone from India had been recorded in 1566. The islands that Columbus believed lay off the cost of Cathay were termed the West Indies, to distinguish them from the islands around the other side of the world, known as the East Indies.

In 1992, five hundred years after Columbus' epic voyage, reactions to the discovery of the Americas by Europeans was mixed. Leaving aside the arguments that suggest that Norwegian sailors had 'discovered' North America centuries before Columbus, by 1992 it was no longer possible simply to celebrate Columbus' 'discovery'; indeed, the terminology of discovery had become problematic. For the discovery of lands inhabited by other civilizations raises fundamental questions about identity, about relationships with place and, as we saw also in the context of the British Isles, about the right to name people, places and things.

Europeans in 1992 could still afford to celebrate the discovery of the New World, which had led to the formation of great empires, and the export of English, French, Spanish and Portuguese to millions of new speakers, but belatedly it has come to be seen that there is also another version of the story. The New World may have been appropriated by the Old, but the native inhabitants of that New World were dispossessed or exterminated in the process. 'Pre-Columbian' has virtually come to signify 'pre-history', for with the arrival of the Europeans, the civilizations of the Americas, their languages and their names, were doomed.

In his study of the relationship between Europeans and native Caribbeans between 1492 and 1727, aptly entitled *Colonial Encounters*, Peter Hulme discusses accounts of the discoveries, citing several respected twentieth-century anthropological and historical works. Questioning the premises upon which scholarly judgements were made, he draws our attention to the assumptions that underlie a great deal of European investigation into non-European cultures:

> What we have, in other words, in texts that claim historical and scientific accuracy, is the elaboration and corroboration of ethnic stereotypes, more powerful for being embedded in contexts which convey a certain amount of historical and ethnographic information. As always, the stereotype operates principally through a judicious combination of adjectives which establish characteristics as external verities immune from the irrelevancies of historical moment: 'ferocious', 'warlike', 'hostile', 'truculent and vindictive' – these are present as innate characteristics irrespective of circumstances; and of course there 'were' cannibals, locked by the verb into a realm of 'beingness' that lies beyond question.[1]

Hulme is here discussing the *Handbook of South American Indians*, published in 1946–50, and draws our attention to the subtle use of emotive language that relies upon stereotypes of savagery. And the savage is, of course, outside the world of civilization, exemplified by the Hellenic world and by Christianity. The early explorers who followed Columbus may have been motivated in many cases by desire for the fabulous wealth that was said to be waiting for them to find, but they carried with them a belief in the civilizing mission of their own culture, a belief which, as Hulme points out, is still enshrined in much European thinking today.

Edmundo O'Gorman, the Mexican historian, talks about the 'invention' of America.[2] Carlos Fuentes, his fellow countryman, expands on this, developing the notion which grew with the European desire for a new, better world, one which would exemplify ideals of civilization. America, he says, was 'discovered because invented because imagined because desired because named'.[3] Humanist intellectuals, he suggests, saw in America the promise of a New Golden Age, and the concept of the Noble Savage was born. But the promise of utopia carried inevitable disappointment:

> We were condemned to utopia by the Old World. What a heavy load! Who could live up to this promise, this demand, this contradiction: to be utopia where utopia was demolished, burned and branded and killed by those who wanted utopia: the epic actors of the Conquest, the awed band of soldiers who entered Tenochtitlán with Cortés in 1519 and discovered the America they had imagined and desired: a New World of enchantment and fantasy only read about before in the romances of chivalry. And who were then forced to destroy what they had named in their dreams of utopia.[4]

If the New World came to be mythologized in terms of a lost dream of utopia, the continent of Africa came to be mythologized in very different ways. The early Portuguese explorers who encountered African civilizations were not motivated by utopian social vision, but by economic goals. African ports were stopovers on the way to the Far East, rather than destinations in their own right, and it is interesting to compare the pattern of European infiltration into the Americas and into Africa. The movement into the interior in both North and South America came quite quickly: Cortés advanced through what is now Mexico, Pizarro through the lands of the Incas in the Andes, the French and English moved rapidly inland from the Eastern seaboard of today's Canada and the United States. In contrast, the movement towards the interior of the African continent came later. As the native populations of the Americas were decimated, an increasing number of slaves were transported across the Atlantic to the expanding settlements and plantations of the Americas. The lucrative slave trade established a pattern of westward movement from Europe and from Africa to the Americas, and gradually the myth of a secret heart of Africa came into being, a place of darkness and fear, in which the gloom of the great forests combined with black skins and suggestions of spirit worship and primeval diabolical powers. Conrad's *Heart of Dark-ness* sums up the European myth of the secret unknown centre of Africa, a myth perpetuated in fiction and the cinema down to the present day.

Wole Soyinka, eminent writer and Professor of Comparative Literature, recounts in his *Myth, Literature and the African World*, his attempts in the early 1970s to give a series of lectures on African literature at Cambridge, where he was Visiting Fellow. His lectures were given under the aegis of the Department of Social Anthropology, for the English Department 'did not believe in any such beast as "African Literature" '.[5] The study of African culture had been classified in a particular way, and the object of that study was anthropological and not literary. Soyinka recognizes this categorization system, and notes that many African universities were also having trouble finding a place for African Literature, the universities having been set up following European models and staffed by European-trained academics.

Soyinka's criticism of the marginalization of African literature is important. He draws attention to the anthropological bias of much European work on Africa, just as Hulme draws our attention to a similar bias in work on Native American languages and cultures. The creation of Centres for African Studies may be a step forward in one respect, but all too often the emphasis has been on social anthropology at the expense of literature. In the 1990s the gap is finally beginning to be bridged somewhat, as post-colonial literary theory emerging from literature departments meets post-colonial anthropology on new territory. And the methodology is essentially comparative.

So long as Europeans tended to relegate the study of non-European cultures to anthropology, and literature departments in Africa tended to teach great European writers, there was little possibility of fresh perspectives. Chidi Amuta feels that there is an ongoing crisis of confidence and of consciousness in current African literary scholarship, even as studies of African literatures and cultures proliferate. This crisis, he argues, derives from the double bind of a lack of definition of African literature, coupled with very precise views on who an African is:

To the Western mind, the African was and has remained a pro-duct of the 'heart of darkness', an incarnation of several racially-defined pathological limitations. To the Western-educated African, on the other hand, the African just happens to be the darkest species of homo sapiens, the victim of centuries of denigration and exploitation.[6]

It is probably fair to say that reaction against the European perspective on African literature led, in the first instance, to an oppositional phase. Ngugi Wa Thiong'O, together with a small group of colleagues, was instrumental in the abolition of the English Department at the University of Nairobi, and the establishment of two broadly-based comparative departments, one for the study of languages and the other for the study of literatures. In his essay 'On the abolition of the English Department', Ngugi argued that by continuing to teach the English tradition in an African context, Africa was turned into an extension of the West. He also refers to the African Renaissance, noting the part played in that trend by Afro-American writers and Caribbean writers. In short, he argued, their aim should be:

> to orient ourselves towards placing Kenya, East Africa, and then Africa in the centre. All other things are to be considered in their relevance to our situation, and their contribution towards understanding ourselves.[7]

Both Ngugi Wa Thiong'O and Chidi Amuta are concerned with what they see as a crisis in African literary scholarship, and both, like Wole Soyinka, find in comparative study a way forward. The confrontational phase of hostility to European influences, traditions and methodologies has turned into an African-centred literary study, in which the impact of Europe on African literature is considered along with other, probably more significant influences, such as the continuation of the vernacular, oral tradition. Nadine Gordimer, endeavouring to define African writing from her perspective as a white African writer argues that:

> African writing is writing done in any language by Africans themselves and by others of whatever skin colour who share with Africans the experience of having been shaped, mentally and spiritually, by Africa rather than anywhere else in the world. One must look at the world *from Africa*, to be an African writer, not look *upon Africa*, from the world.[8]

These African writers propose an Africa-centred consciousness, and a study of literature that starts with Africa and considers other literatures in relation to that African centre. This model of comparative literature is in complete contrast to the old Eurocentric models that rejected comparison with non-European texts on the grounds of unbridgeable difference and the absence of a place in the western canon.

If African comparatists can be sure of their starting point, having renamed their literature departments in such a way as to abolish the pre-eminence of English and other European languages, where does this leave European comparatists? The African reaction to what Chinua Achebe has called 'colonialist criticism', marked by its belief in the excellence of the literary products of the Hellenic and Judaeo-Christian world, has led, at times, to an aggressively self-assertive stance and to heated debate among African critics at different points along the spectrum of resistance to European models. It has even been suggested that only Africans can study African literature, a premise that, if universally applicable, would effectively ban any critic from studying any text written outside his or her own culture. As Jahnheinz Jahn comments, critics of African literature have tended to be 'racists, nationalists or individualists'.[9] So at the one extreme we might have a European perspective that refuses to recognize African literature and conceives of African Studies as purely anthropological, while at the other extreme, we might have an African perspective that refutes the influence of any European literary models along with a rejection of colonialism *per se*.

Despite these polarizations (and unhappily, there *are* still some scholars who belong to each of these hypothetical camps of extremists), work that is currently developing that looks comparatively at post-colonial cultures and their literary production offers a way forward for former colonized and colonizers alike. As Ashcroft *et al.* put it:

> Post-colonial literary theory has begun to deal with the problems of transmuting time into space, with the present struggling out of the past, and, like much recent post-colonial literature, it attempts to construct a future. The post-colonial world is one in which destructive cultural encounter is changing into an acceptance of difference on equal terms. Both literary theorists and cultural historians are beginning to recognize cross-culturality as the potential termination

point of an apparently endless human history of conquest and annihilation . . . the strength of post-colonial theory may well lie in its inherently comparative methodology and the hybridized and syncretic view of the modern world which this implies.[10]

The arrival of the term 'post-colonial' on the critical scene must surely be one of the most significant developments in comparative literature in the twentieth century. Once we take on board the term, geographical entities shift, and other considerations come to the fore. If we consider post-colonialism in diachronic terms, then the long struggle of North and South American writers in the eighteenth and nineteenth centuries to create their own literatures can be compared to the struggle of contemporary African and Latin American writers to do the same. And the whole question of what constitutes one's 'own' literature is also debatable. What is an American? asked Crèvecoeur in 1782,[11] when the problem of definition after the revolution of 1776 was still so crucial, and two centuries later the Mexican, Carlos Fuentes, follows the Cuban, Alejo Carpentier, in declaring that the task of an American writer is to baptize things that would otherwise be nameless.[12] Significantly, both Fuentes and Carpentier cross cultures biographically: Fuentes grew up as the son of a Mexican diplomat in the United States, while Carpentier, years in Paris influenced him profoundly.

The theme of exile, of belonging and non-belonging, is a common link between writers from post-colonial cultures. Equally, the problematics of language and national identity offers another fundamental point of unity. So, for example, along with a rejection of the canon of English literature, comes a rejection of a British-based Standard English, and the same process can be seen happening to other European languages in post-colonial societies, alongside a reappraisal of native vernaculars. This means that there is a multiplicity of horizons of expectation according to the linguistic starting point of the reader; hence a European reading a poem by a Caribbean writer like Jean Binta Breeze or a novel by an African writer like Amos Tutuola will encounter an unfamiliar lexicon and syntax, in contrast to a reader who shares an understanding of these linguistic signs with the author.

Comparison of forms and content across post-colonial literatures offers a wealth of possibilities. Equally important is the linked question of the comparative history of post-colonial literatures, for as has already been pointed out, it is European cultural history that has for so long provided a model. So the twin periods of the Renaissance and Romanticism are used by European critics as measuring posts, and periodization hinges on these and other moments of transition. This traditional method of periodization has all kinds of implications. For example, if we take Hellenic culture as a high point of Western civilization, and the Roman Empire as a continuation (diluted) of that Hellenic ideal, we end up with a long period of several centuries following the collapse of the Roman empire that is termed 'the Dark Ages'. Conventional European periodization sees the Roman Empire as a phase of enlightenment, albeit a somewhat aggressive one, followed by a descent into darkness and anarchy, revived in the twelfth century by the spread of monasticism and the creation of universities across Europe (the Middle Ages). This period then spans several more centuries, until the arrival of the Renaissance somewhere in the fourteenth and fifteenth centuries, depending on where you are standing when noticing it.

It is remarkable that such a bizarre division of cultural history should have lasted for so long. As was pointed out in chapter 3, the glory of Irish monasticism was only one of the developments that gives the lie to the myth of centuries of 'darkness'. But most significantly of all, during the so-called Dark Ages, civilizations flourished in other parts of the world, particularly in those parts adjacent to Europe, in what is now the Middle East and North Africa. That there was a great leap forward in European societies in the fields of architecture, mathematics, medicine, music, poetry, philosophy, etc. in the twelfth century is undeniable, but what has been denied and all but erased is the enormous influence of the Arab world on that process of development.

Again, in the high Renaissance, at that point in time hailed by Europeans as one of the great moments of civilization, in the very year that Columbus set out on his first trans-Atlantic voyage, Spain expelled its Jewish population and drove out the last of the Arabs by conquering the Moorish kingdom of Granada, a final gesture in the centuries of conflict between Christian and non-Christian, during which all the beneficial aspects of contact with the Arab world were signally ignored. The Renaissance may be perceived as a moment of extraordinary aesthetic richness, but it was also an age of political and religious intolerance and the age that saw the start of the evils of colonial expansion outside Europe.

Small wonder, then, that there should be such resistance to the traditional European periodization model, when it either bears little relationship to anything that happened outside a fairly narrowly circumscribed geographical boundary or is based on totally different premises which ignore non-European realities. Comparatists from China, from India, from African and Latin American contexts are uniting in refuting the European model of cultural periodization, replacing it with their own alternative models. This movement is yet another example of the ways in which the old ideas of the universality of literature and of literary history are being challenged.

Post-colonialism is quite distinct from anti-colonialism. Reactions against colonialism have manifested themselves in a variety of ways, but always posited on the premise of a binary opposition. Where post-colonialism differs, is that although challenging the hegemony of colonizing cultures, it recognizes the plurality of contacts between colonizing and colonized. Of particular importance in furthering post-colonial theory has been the growth of literatures produced in bilingual or multilingual mixed-race societies since the 1950s.

Ashcroft *et al.* feel the Caribbean has been the 'crucible of the most extensive and challenging post-modern theory'.[13] This is a strong claim, though perhaps unduly partisan. Of comparable importance has been the developing consciousness of bilingual communities in Canada and the United States, which has accelerated since the early 1960s and resulted in a rich literature, cinema and music culture. The rise to prominence of Chicano literature in particular has powerful implications for both North and South American cultures.

The differences between Caribbean societies and the Chicanos are all too apparent: the history of the Caribbean, from the time of Columbus' first arrival, has been a history of genocide, brutal slave trading, economic exploitation, poverty and racism. Once the native populations were all but wiped out, black slaves were shipped over like cattle to work on the plantations, and even after the abolition of slavery, which happened at very different points across the Caribbean as a whole, the exploitation of poor immigrant workers from Asia continued. The history of the Chicanos, on the contrary, is one of dispossession, racism and exploitation, and there are many similarities, as the early members of the Chicano civil rights movement point out, between the treatment of native Hispanics in the United States and the treatment of Native Americans.

The common link between Chicanos and the population of the Caribbean is their cultural and racial hybridization. This is a point that has been repeatedly stressed by such prominent writers as Wilson Harris, Edward Brathwaite, George Lamming, Tomás Rivera, Rudolfo Anaya or Alurista. Recognizing that there is no single identity, no common ancestral line but rather a plethora of races and of cultures, means that the Caribbean or Chicano concept of history is a flexible one. As George Lamming puts it in *The Pleasures of Exile* (1960) he is a descendant of both colonizers and colonized:

> For I am a direct descendant of slaves, too near to the actual enterprise to believe that its echoes are over with the reign of emancipation. Moreover, I am a direct descendant of Prospero, working in the same temple of endeavour, using his legacy of language – not to curse our meeting – but to push it further, reminding the descendants of both sides that what's done is done, and can only be seen as a soil from which other gifts, or the same gift endowed with different meanings, may grow towards a future which is colonized by our acts at this moment, but which must always remain open.[14]

Rodolfo Gonzalez explores a similar dilemma in his long poem, *I am Joaquín* (*Yo soy Joaquín*), published, like so many Chicano texts, in both English and Spanish. In his introduction to the 1967 edition, he explains the sources of his work:

> *I am Joaquín* became a historical essay, a social statement, a conclusion of our *mestisaje*, a welding of the oppressor (Spaniard) and the oppressed (Indian). It is a mirror of our greatness and our weakness, a call to action as a total people, emerging from a glorious history, travelling through social pain and conflicts, confessing our weaknesses while we shout about our strength, culminating into one: the psychological wounds, cultural genocide, social castration, nobility, courage, determination, and the fortitude to move on to make new history for an ancient people dancing on a modern stage.[15]

Both Lamming and Gonzalez, in their different ways, are seeking to come to terms with the history of their people and to move forward into the future. Spaniard and Indian, black slave and white colonizer are the ancestors of the new mixed races of the present. There is no sense here of polarization, rather recognition of the multifaceted nature of Chicano or Caribbean cultures. Gonzalez' poem, which was one of the first texts to be published for Chicanos by a Chicano writer, is a highly ambitious work. It attempts a history of the Chicanos, tracing their ancestry back through the story of the migrant workers of California and the southwestern states, the Mexican revolution, the struggle against Spanish colonial rule, the arrival of the Conquistadores and the pre-Columbian Aztec and Maya empires. At each stage in the history of the Chicanos, he points to the contradictions of being descended from both oppressor and oppressed. So at the start of the poem, Joaquín claims he is both 'the sword and the flame of Cortés . . . and the eagle and serpent of the Aztec civilization', and later that he is 'both tyrant and slave', while the poem ends with the lines:

> I am Aztec prince and Christian Christ.
> I SHALL ENDURE !
> I WILL ENDURE !

What will unite Chicanos, members of *La Raza*, as the early Chicano movement referred to themselves, is being able to take a stand against the discrimination they suffer in time present at the hands of what is described as the 'Anglo success' of the United States, combined with an awareness of who they are and where they come from. Gonzalez presents Chicanos with an uncomfortable picture of centuries of compromise and collusion, that stands alongside the other picture of their ancestors as victims of oppression and enslavement. He notes, with some bitterness, that the history of Chicanos is stained with blood, much of it shed for the same society that discriminates against them:

> My blood runs pure on the ice-caked
> hills of the Alaskan isles,
> on the corpse-strewn beach of Normandy,
> the foreign land of Korea
> > and now
> > Vietnam.

George Lamming describes his mixed ancestry (his home island is Barbados) through references to Shakespeare's play, *The Tempest*, and Peter Hulme discusses the importance this text has acquired in the post-colonial context.[16] For there is a fundamental ambiguity in the play: Prospero, the dispossessed Duke who has been exiled with his daughter Miranda to the island, has magical powers that enable him to compel the inhabitants of that island, the spirit Ariel and the monster Caliban, to do his bidding. Caliban, whose name, as countless readers have noted, can be read as an anagram of 'can(n)ibal', is the character to whom the most beautiful language in the play has been given, but is also the character who plots Prospero's death and the rape of Miranda. So we have a double perspective, either of a benevolent master who has endeavoured to civilize the brutish creature he has taken into his service, only to be repaid by ingratitude, or of a native inhabitant deprived of his inheritance by an outsider and forced into slavery. And when Miranda reminds Caliban of how she and her father had found him, 'a thing most brutish', unable to speak and know his own meaning, he replies:

> You taught me language, and my profit on't
> Is I know how to curse. The red plague rid you
> For learning me your language. (I.ii.366–8)

Peter Hulme reminds us that Prospero's magical powers are not nearly so great as Caliban imagines them to be. He can exercise his magic on the island, but not off it (he was, after all, deposed and exiled against his will, unable to prevent it happening) and he needs the services of the islanders in order to survive. Hulme compares this state of affairs to the situation of Europeans in America in the seventeenth century, when the strength of their firearms made them appear to be magicians, but who were unable to feed themselves. He notes that this

> is a topos that appears with remarkable frequency in the early English colonial narratives, as it had in the Spanish: a group of Europeans who were dependent . . . for many years, on food supplied by their native hosts, often willingly, sometimes under duress.[17]

Conquerors, colonizers, guests, settlers – the terminology varies with different perspectives. George Lamming claims he 'cannot read *The Tempest* without recalling those voyages reported by Hakluyt.' Thinking of *The Tempest* reminds him inexorably of English colonialism, and he argues that the play was also prophetic 'of a political future which is our present'. Taught the language of the newcomers and simultaneously enslaved by them, his ancestors passed on their ambiguity to their descendants, so that for Lamming 'the circumstances of my life, both as a colonial and exiled descendant of Caliban in the twentieth century, is an example of that prophecy.'[18] Coming to terms with the past means facing the ambiguities of a plural history, and both Lamming and Gonzalez draw our attention to the multifariousness of their different cultural heritages. There can be no clearly-defined point of origin, no exact source, and as a result no polarization between binary opposites. What remains is the need to recognize the complexities of the historical processes that have resulted in such pluralism.

For the Caribbean George Lamming, the threads in the web run back through to Africa and to Europe. For Rodolfo Gonzalez, they run back through to Native American civilizations and to Europe, but extended now to considerations of north and south. Chicanos are by definition of mixed racial origins, and the possessors of a dual linguistic background, English and Spanish. As Chicano literature has developed, so the question of the categorization of it has become problematic, and although to some extent categorization presents difficulties when we consider how to define 'Caribbean' literature, the situation is different. Wilson Harris can be described as a Caribbean writer because his work focuses on the transformative power of his own multicultural inheritance, whilst García Márquez, whose work can be interestingly compared to that of Harris and who was born in the Colombian Caribbean hinterland, sees himself as a Latin American rather than as a Caribbean writer.[19]

The Caribbean as a geographical and historical entity superimposes itself over the linguistic, ethnic and religious differences of the peoples within its boundaries. The case of Chicano culture is more problematic, for there is no geographical entity, no homeland, despite the idealistic claims in the late 1960s for the mystical nation of Aztlan. Chicano writing is outside mainstream Mexican literature, and equally outside mainstream United States literature, and as Octavio Paz pointed out in *The Labyrinth of Solitude*, the Chicano neither wants to return to a Mexican origin, nor blend into North American society.[20]

Chicano literature can be said to have developed not out of any sense of a 'return' to anything, for there was no point of origin in the first place, but rather from a desire to establish an identity, to speak out and have that voice heard. There is a good deal of debate about precisely when that literature came into being (there are several claimants for the 'first Chicano novel' category), but it is probably fair to say that apart from isolated examples of written texts and a flourishing oral song and poetry tradition, Chicano literary texts began to proliferate in the 1960s, when Chicano politics came onto the agenda alongside the Civil Rights movements which empowered Black and Native Americans. From small beginnings came a rush of novels, poetry, plays, Chicano publishing houses, university departments, radio and TV stations, representation on the MLA and international Chicano Studies associations.

This proliferation of texts has altered Chicano literature from within, besides giving it a much higher profile in the world outside. Chicano consciousness began in the 1960s with direct political activity, with César Chavez and the National Farm Workers' Association strike against the California wine producers. The Delano grape strike which began in 1965 and went on for six years brought the plight of the migrant Mexican workers (from first to fifth generation) to the attention of a world-wide audience. Luis Valdez, the great Chicano theatre practitioner, created his *Actos* on the picket lines, while Tomás Rivera's cyclical collection of stories, *Y no se lo tragó la tierra* (And the earth did not part) offers an account of the lives of the field labourers in ways which recall Joyce's *Dubliners*, in terms of structure, tone and narrative voice.

Since the 1960s Chicano Studies has entered the curriculum and there are now a whole variety of methods and theoretical approaches, some of which are a long way removed from the beginnings of the Chicano movement with its roots in working class politics. Chicano literature has also changed, moving from attempts to create a Chicano 'epic' poem and novels depicting the deprivations suffered by migrant workers to more complex narrative and poetic structures. Gender issues have also come to the fore, as in the Caribbean context, and there is now a Chicana literature of growing importance. More particularly, however, there is the phenomenon of bilingualism, and of bilingual poetry especially.

Bilingual writing is an ancient phenomenon, and happens whenever there are readers able to shift easily between languages. For
Chicano readers, with their Spanish and English background, and
the development of *pocho*, the dialect of Spanish spoken by Chicanos
and heavily influenced by the grammar and lexicon of English,
bilingual poetry offers exciting transcultural possibilities.

One of the greatest Chicano poets, Alurista, writes in a mixture
of English and Spanish that assumes equal linguistic skills in shifting
cultures from his readers. His poetry draws upon a variety of
traditions, from Nahuatl poetry, Mexican poetry – pre-Columbian
and Spanish, from contemporary pop culture, from the Catholic
litany, from the beat poets, using literary and oral sources, blending
languages, creating neologisms. This kind of poetry is genuinely
innovative, yet relies upon a range of traditions, all of which are
absorbed into the writing. There is no single source, no dominant
tradition: the multiple nature of Chicano history results in a multiple
type of text.

We can see a similar process at work in some Caribbean writers.
In the 1930s, the Cuban Nicolás Guillén, for example, in his collections *Motivos de son*, and *Sóngoro cosongo*, created 'sound'
poems, working with a combination of Spanish ballads, African
rhythms and Black dance music. Likewise Alejo Carpentier, the
Cuban novelist, wrote his *Ecue-Yamba-O* in 1933 at the age of 29,
a short novel that drew upon Afro-Cuban music for its inspiration.
Years later, in *The Lost Steps* (1949), Carpentier's autobiographical
protagonist who goes back in time and into his own soul is a
musicologist, led to the primeval forests of his origins ostensibly by
the search for a primitive instrument.

Guillén and Carpentier wrote in Spanish; the Francophone poet
Aimé Césaire drew, like them, upon African song rhythms, attempting to recreate a lost ancestral heritage, and in the process trans-
forming a European language through the use of non-European
rhythmical patterns. But Césaire's Africanness and the concept of
'Négritude' he espoused, Négritude as an assertion of blackness and
of the triumph of the African spirit through centuries of oppression
is, in a way, comparable to what Fuentes sees as the imposition of
utopian ideals upon the new world by the first Europeans. Nadine
Gordimer argues that despite their desire to see themselves as a
continuation of an African past:

all that was left of Africa to the Caribbean writers was the colour of their skin. And unlike the Jews, their identity had been fragmented in slave plantations instead of concentrated within the ghetto.[21]

But she also recognizes the impact of the dream Africa of the Caribbean writers upon African writers:

> The Caribbean negro writer's dream of home – of a home never experienced, never seen – created modern African literature because it placed before Africans a new valuation of African life as a positive entity instead of a negation measured against the white man's way of life.[22]

Gordimer suggests that the Caribbean idealization of Africa offered in turn a model image to Africans, that stood in stark contrast to the image of Africa as the heart of darkness. Moreover, Césaire's poetry in its use of psychic landscapes accords more closely with African notions of the inter-relationship between man and his environment than with the European tradition of the poet who is inspired by the contemplation of nature.

There has been a great deal of debate amongst African and Caribbean scholars about the ideological implications of Négritude. Wole Soyinka recognizes the importance of Négritude in terms of its idealistic vision of Africa and African culture, but argues that it was a grossly over-simplified vision. He criticizes Leopold Senghor for suggesting that whilst Europeans employ analytical thought, Africans are more intuitive, on the grounds that this supposition is still based on 'the Manichean tradition of European thought'[23] and argues that:

> Négritude trapped itself in what was primarily a defensive role, even though its accents were strident, its syntax hyperbolic and its strategy aggressive. It accepted one of the most commonplace blasphemies of racism, that the black man has nothing between his ears, and proceeded to subvert the power to poetry to glorify this fabricated justification of European cultural domination ... The fundamental error was one of procedure: Négritude stayed within a pre-set system of Eurocentric intellectual analysis, both of man and society, and tried to re-define the African and his society in those externalized terms.[24]

As soon as we start to consider great generalized categories such as European/African/Asian/Latin American literary systems, we enter a labyrinth of corridors, with mirrors that reflect or distort, doors that have never been opened, closed rooms and dead ends. The comparatist is drawn into the labyrinth, for it offers an infinite wealth of altered perceptions and innovative connections. A comparative literature that starts with the high canon of European culture offers precisely defined pathways, roads with markers along which the scholar can travel safely between predetermined periods, styles and literary conventions. But the labyrinth offers so many more possibilities. What it does not offer are clear-cut answers and definitions. In this respect, the comparative labyrinth opened by post-colonial theories of literary production is much more in keeping with the pluralism of the post-modernist world of the 1990s. The old positivist notion of the road along which cultures marched towards Progress ultimately leads nowhere.

If Eurocentric concepts of comparative literary study have been confined and constrained by the need to keep on known tracks and not stray off the map of Hellenic/Christian culture, that need is not shared by scholars starting from a different point. The principle problem for writers and scholars in Latin America or in Africa, for example, has been to find ways of articulating their perceptions of their own cultural products in relation to the products of other cultures, particularly when those other cultures have also been their masters in all senses of the term. Hence the need for Négritude at the same time as the need to refute Négritude; the need for Chicano writers to see themselves as Latinos while simultaneously refusing to be located within Mexican literary tradition.

In 1982 García Márquez was awarded the Nobel Prize for Literature. In his Nobel Address, he tackled the question of the tasks of the Latin American writer, looking at the extraordinary history of his continent, from the first travellers' tales through to Pablo Neruda, whose death came shortly after the coup which murdered the president of Chile in 1973. Commenting upon the monstrous poverty and the continuous political oppression of much of Latin America, he also refers to the dangers of seeking to interpret these horrors from a European perspective, seeing Latin America as 'underdeveloped' without regard to the history of atrocities in Europe or to the responsibility of Europeans in forging the chains that bind other cultures. His address opens with reference to one of the many accounts of voyages to the New World, which combines lurid fantasy with precisely detailed scientific data:

> Antonio Pignafetta, the Florentine navigator who accompanied Magellan on his first circumnavigation of the world, kept a meticulous log on his journey through our Southern American continent which, nevertheless, also seems to be an adventure into the imagination. He related that he had seen pigs with their umbilicus in their backs and birds without feet, the females of the species of which would brood their eggs on the backs of the males, as well as others like gannets without tongues whose beaks looked like a spoon. He wrote that he had seen a monstrosity of an animal with the head and ears of a mule, the body of a camel, the hooves of a deer and the neigh of a horse. He related that they put a mirror in front of the first native they met in Patagonia and how that overexcited giant lost the use of his reason out of fear of his own image.[25]

The early travellers sought to describe the new with the perceptual tools and literary conventions of the known world. So they drew upon a hoard of images of mythical beasts, tales of the unknown and imaginary worlds, as exemplified in the hugely popular romances of chivalry. These images of a fantasy come to life, combined with the desire to believe in the existence of Utopia and the 'noble savage' shaped European perceptions of Latin America. Gradually, as the utopian ideals faded, the continent came to signify something alien, one of the last places on earth. Even today, myths of Latin America prevailing in Europe and the United States see the continent as the place to which criminals, bank robbers or ex-Nazis can run and hide, the place down below from which dark hordes of illegal immigrants, drug traffickers, killer bees and other undesirable diabolic things seek to rise up and cross the Rio Grande into the light of western civilization.

    García Márquez rejects such myth-making, even whilst acknowledging that the reality of Latin America is just as fantastical as the stories it generates. The task facing a Latin American writer is to find ways of talking about that reality, without having to resort to the models laid down by what he terms with irony 'venerable old Europe'. Nevertheless, the two writers he acknowledges as outstanding are Neruda and William Faulkner, referred to as his master. García Márquez recognizes the simultaneous need for the creation of a new writing that will reflect the new reality, whilst at the same time acknowledging that the history of Latin America cannot be separated from that of Europe and the rest of the world. Latin America, he argues, is not the shadow of a European dream. Its realities are quite different from those of Europe, lived and experienced differently and depicted differently by its writers.

García Márquez is renowned for the ways in which he combines realism with fantasy in what has come to be termed 'magical realism'. Carpentier had earlier talked about 'the real in the marvellous', and Borges has shown consistently how easily the boundaries between rational and anti-rational universes can be transgressed by a writer looking from a new perspective. In his homage to Borges after his death in 1986, Octavio Paz says:

> Europeans were surprised at the universality of Borges, but none of them realized that this cosmopolitanism was, and could only be, the point of view of a Latin American . . . A non-European way. Both inside and outside the European tradition, the Latin American can see the West as a totality, and not with the fatally provincial vision of the French, the German, the English or the Italian.[26]

Paz's reference to European provincialism recalls Kavanagh's distinction between the parochial and the provincial in Irish writing, discussed in chapter 3. This parallel is a good one, because it serves to revise notions of Europe as the centre, with everyone else out in the provinces – the classic imperial model of ancient Rome that has been absorbed so profoundly by later civilizations. So Ovid, for example, wrote his *Tristia* as a lament against his fate of being condemned to exile away from the centre, out into what he perceived as the margins of Empire. That aspect of the theme of exile, of being banished to the provinces away from the place upon which all eyes are directed is common to many European writers, but outside Europe it alters significantly. A comparative study of themes and images of exile as used by Chinese, European or Caribbean writers, for example, would produce some interesting diversities. Kavanagh points out quite rightly, that the provincial perspective is always looking elsewhere, seeing the centre that is denied, whilst the parochial view turns inwards and in consequence becomes universal. Parochialism owes nothing to a centre that is somewhere else. Anywhere else simply ceases to be important.

The development of magical realism in Latin American fiction can be traced back to the multiple perceptions of reality inherited from the pre-Columbian period and from the colonial past. The creatures of fantasy depicted by the early European voyagers became superimposed upon the mythical beasts of the ancient pre-Columbian pantheons; the excesses of tyrants and corrupt politicians have been blended together with stories of saints and martyrs from the Catholic Christian tradition; scientific knowledge and impossible fantasies sit side by side on the page. García Márquez's novel *Autumn of the Patriarch* (1976) fuses historical information about generations of different dictators with horrific excesses created in his own imagination, and Roa Bastos' *I, the Supreme One* (1974) also combines fact and fantasy with absurd and terrifying power. Latin American writers frequently point to the difficulties in drawing clear lines between the real and the fantastic, and indeed their writing compels us to rethink that terminology. What are we to make of a novel like Luisa Valenzuela's *The Lizard's Tale* (1983), for example, which depicts the terror of Argentina in the 1970s using techniques of surrealist narrative, with the writer appearing as a character in her own book? And the story of how the British smuggled rubber plants out of Brazil to set up their own lucrative plantations in South East Asia, thereby destroying the astonishing wealth of the Amazonian rubber planters, who had even built opera houses and palaces on land cleared in the jungle by enslaved Indians, is so fantastical it belongs more to expectations of fiction than of history.

The blending of cultures, however brutally begun, has produced the many different societies of Africa, Latin America and the Caribbean today, and the evidence of that complex web of cultural threads is to be found in the literatures of those regions. Magical realism has come to be used by European critics to describe a great deal of writing from other parts of the world, not only Latin America – but also Indian writing, or Turkish, or Czech or Roumanian or Nigerian – wherever novelists appear to be rejecting the boundaries of the realist mode of fiction.

Magical realism involves the reader in a perceptual leap across systems. Edward Brathwaite, the Caribbean writer, reiterates Carlos Fuentes' statements about the task of the writer being that of naming the new world of their post-colonial reality, and he sees that process of naming as being similar to a quest:

In the Caribbean, whether it be African or Amerindian, the recognition of an ancestral relationship with the folk of aboriginal culture involves the artist and participant in a journey into the past and hinterland which is at the same time a movement of possession into present and future. Through this movement of possession we become ourselves, truly our own creators, discovering word for object, image for word.[27]

The movement of possession involves coming to terms with history, it involves finding a voice, naming things. It also involves showing the rest of the world what has happened along the way, and here we find that alongside narrative developments that can be loosely termed 'magical realist', is a strong tradition of 'realist narrative', that exposes the full horrors of the colonial past and its legacy for the present. A great deal of Chicano literature, for example, is concerned with depicting the plight of Chicano farm workers, peasants, urban slum dwellers and dislocated adolescents. Reflecting on the state of the Chicano novel, Joseph Sommers suggests that comparative cultural study might consider the work of a major novelist such as Tomás Rivera, alongside that of other writers such as Robert Musil, J. D. Salinger, Richard Wright or Mario Vargas Llosa.[28] To which list we might add, very obviously, Chinua Achebe, for both Rivera and Achebe write about the impact of the colonial past upon the present, thereby simultaneously exposing social injustice and seeking to restore the pride of Chicano or African peoples in themselves. And the realism of many African novelists, like many Chicanos, can be arguably said to be a reaction against the dismissive romanticization of Africans or Mexican Americans in colonial literature. Significantly, a great many post-colonial realist novels have children or adolescents as protagonists, so that the reader's journey follows the progress of that child through stages of discovery, frequently through a descending spiral of disillusionment.

Post-colonial comparative literature is also a voyage of discovery, only this time, instead of the European setting off in search of riches and new lands to conquer, equipped with maps and charts to aid him, this voyage is one towards self-awareness, towards recognition of responsibility, guilt, complicity and collusion in the creation of the labyrinthine world of contemporary writing. Europeans are no longer embarking on that voyage from the centre of the world either, for centres and peripheries have been redefined. The English novel, which would have sunk without trace into genteel provincial decay, has been brought back to life by the vitality of novelists writing in English who have never been to Britain and have little or no interest in going there. George Lamming sums up what has been happening:

> There is a tendency to speak of colonialism as though it were exclusively a black experience. That is a very limited understanding. It was a two-way thing. Colonialism has been as much a white experience as a black one. It is simply that it has taken the white world a very long time to understand the nature of that enterprise . . .[29]

Comparative literary study in the 1990s will have to work with the recognition of colonialism and all its implications as having been, indeed, a two-way thing.

5
Constructing Cultures:
the Politics of Travellers' Tales

Michel Foucault has suggested that there are only two forms of comparison: the comparison of measurement, which 'analyses into units in order to establish relations of equality and inequality' and that of order, which establishes the simplest elements and arranges differences.[1] Comparative literary study has tended in the past to be overly concerned with the first type of comparison, setting up canons of primary and secondary authors, greater and lesser texts, stronger and weaker cultures, majority and minority languages, and trying hard to keep the ideological implications of such hierarchization out of sight. Only latterly has there been a shift towards the second type of comparison, and one of the most significant developments of more recent comparative literary study involves a change in our readings of accounts of journeys, of the diaries, letters, translations and tales told by travellers of their experiences of other cultures.

Columbus' account of his voyages to the New World is full, as Todorov has pointed out, of references to the magic word 'oro' (*gold*).[2] Where gold failed to materialize, he proceeded further, driven by the certainty that it must be there, just out of reach. Other colonizers expressed their journeys in terms of land cultivation, planting and fertilizing, hoeing, tilling, ploughing the land, and recently scholars have begun to point out the equation of this kind of imagery with that of rape.[3] The virgin colony lying back and waiting to be 'husbanded' is a pornographic fantasy that recurs through the accounts of Europeans seeking their fortunes overseas, and the very name of the American colony Virginia seemed to inspire a considerable number of lewd metaphors.

Contemporary readings of accounts of travels, inspired by differing methodologies deriving from gender studies, cultural studies and post-modernist theory, expose subtexts beneath the apparently innocent details of journeys in other lands that enable us to see more clearly the ways in which travellers construct the cultures they experience. From travellers' accounts of their journeys, we can trace the presence of cultural stereotypes, and the way in which an individual reacts to what is seen elsewhere can reflect tendencies in the traveller's home culture. So, for example, Jane Austen's contemporary, Mr. J. B. Scott of Bungay, Suffolk (1792–1828) first travelled to France and Italy in 1814, and predictably his journals are full of anecdotes about Napoleon, together with details on the meals he enjoyed on his journey. He also gives us statements about the landscape and the people, and the following extract gives a sense of the tone of his writing:

> The women of Leghorn are singularly fair in general, much to our surprise, for their neighbours of Provence are almost mulattoes. They wear a kind of white veil hanging from the top of their heads, and descending over their shoulders, which looks very pretty. Their earrings are generally of immense size. The Tuscan men are a fine intelligent set of people. Their hatred for the French is fully equalled by that they entertain for the Austrians.[4]

Scott follows the fashion of a young English intellectual of his day and like Byron and Shelley, supports Italian independence claims from Austria. He is also, as a young man just down from Cambridge, interested in women, commenting regularly on the clothes and appearance of women he observed on his travels. But there is an anthropological note to this account of the women and men of Leghorn, that transforms them into objects, creatures who acquire substance because he bestows it upon them. The women have unusually large earrings and pretty headgear; the men are fine and intelligent. What he sees and what he assumes are blurred, and his own English patriotism finds its counterpart in what he confidently assures us is hatred for the French who at that point in time were commonly seen as the devils of Europe. Scott moves from the descriptive mode to statements of certainty with the confidence of the traveller who knows he is in a position of authority vis-à-vis his subjects. A product of his age, middle class, well-educated and undertaking the classic Grand Tour of his contemporaries, Scott typifies a particular type of man travelling at a particular moment in time. His journals are therefore not only the idiosyncratic production of a single individual, they are representative of the society from which he came. Significantly, they were published in 1930 under the title *An Englishman at Home and Abroad, 1792–1828*. A century after his death, J. B. Scott's editor, Ethel Mann, was characterizing him as 'An Englishman'. Moreover, the foreword to the edition of the journals was written by none other than Lilias Rider Haggard, widow of Sir Henry Rider Haggard, author of *King Solomon's Mines* and *She* and a host of other highly successful popular novels about the virtues of imperial rule and the greatness of the Englishman abroad.

We can indeed learn a great deal from accounts of travels, and this may yet prove to be one of the most fruitful areas for comparative study that has come to light in recent years. Moreover, an examination of the varied texts produced by travellers shows how prejudices, stereotypes and negative perceptions of other cultures can be handed down through generations.

Accounts of journeys can also show us other things about the way in which travellers perceive their place in the world they inhabit.

Let us take another, very different example from another age, an account of a journey by a perhaps untypical Englishman, though equally a product of his own time.

On Saturday 21 September 1583 Dr John Dee, mathematician, philosopher, map-maker and astrologer to Queen Elizabeth I, left England, accompanied by his assistant Edward Kelley and their families, to travel to Cracow in Poland. They took ship from Gravesend and, as detailed in *A True and Faithful Relation of what passed for many years between Dr. John Dee . . . and Some Spirits*[5] followed a circuitous path via Amsterdam, up the Zuider Zee to Harlingen and then in a series of small boats crossing short stretches of water until they came to Embden on 17 October. Communicating with spirits at different places where they rested, they proceeded on to Bremen, and thence across to Lübeck, finally reaching Stettin on Christmas Day. It had taken them three months, travelling through a remarkable range of places, by boat and overland, but it then took them only four days to travel over 200 miles down to Posen, despite the rigors of winter. Eventually, on 13 March 1584, the travellers reached their destination. Dee notes where they lodged in Cracow and furthermore that:

Master Edward Kelley came to us on Fryday in the Easter week by the new Gregorian Kalendar, being the 27 day of March by the old Kalendar, but the sixth day of April by the new Kalendar, Easter Day being the first day of April in Poland, by the new Gregorian institution.

Dee took great care to record both the old style of dates and the new once he had arrived in Poland, for although the Gregorian calendar was very recent, it had been adopted throughout Catholic Europe, and scholars from Protestant countries, although refusing to accept what was considered as a papist reform (the Gregorian calendar was not accepted in England until 1752) were nevertheless extremely interested. Dee had written an unpublished discourse to the Queen in February 1538, inviting her to 'peruse and consider as concerning the needful Reformation of the Vulgar Kalendar for the civil years and daies accompting or veryfying, according to the time truly spent',[6] and the question of calendar reform was clearly an important factor in his travels across northern Europe and sojourn in Cracow, Prague and Trebon in Southern Bohemia.

Dee's interest in calendar reform marks a shift in his scientific work that appears to coincide with his meeting with Edward Kelley (who served as his medium in the summoning of spirits) and his departure from England for central Europe. In the 1570s a great deal of Dee's time had been spent on map-making, advising such travellers as Martin Frobisher, who was seeking a north-western passage to Cathay, and Sir Francis Drake, who sailed around the world in the years between 1577 and 1580. Dee had previously, in the 1550s, advised on the early voyages to try and find a north-east passage to Cathay, and published his *General and Rare Memorials pertayning to the Perfect Arte of Navigation* in 1577. Peter French, Dee's biographer, noting that the two central sections of this work are missing, possibly because they contained politically sensitive material, points out that Dee was preoccupied with the establishment of an 'incomparable British Empire'.[7] Dee was a product of the great age of voyages of discovery, the moment when map-making became a science rather than an art, when the map became an instrument of hegemony, the means by which whole civilizations could be conquered, millions of slaves traded across oceans and whole patterns of social relations altered irrevocably. As Mary Hamer says, map-making signifies a process of massive change:

the very activities of measuring, ordering, regulating and standard-
izing, the production of accuracy that is the prerequisite of scale
mapping, involve a rigorous shaping of the material world that is at
odds with and alien to the forms in which the material world has its
prior existence.[8]

But Dee moved away from map-making, shifted his focus to the
problem of measuring time and dates and turned his attention to
making contact with the anti-material world of the spirits, a shift
that has troubled generations of scholars unable to reconcile mathematics, map-making and magic in the manner of Dee's contemporaries. Not that all his contemporaries were able to effect such
a reconciliation either: John Foxe, for example, referred to him as
'the great Conjurer' and 'a Caller of Divils',[9] terms of abuse that
provoked Dee so much he demanded a public withdrawal.

The principle puzzle for a twentieth-century reader of Dee's
account of his journey to Cracow, however, is why he should have
taken such a seemingly tortuous route. But if we construct a map of
religious differences in Europe in the sixteenth century, and pages
38–9 of *Muir's Historical Atlas* provide just such a map, colour
coded, then it becomes apparent that Dee and his party had carefully
steered a course through Calvinist and Lutheran territories, avoid-
ing Catholic-dominated lands, making their way down from the
Baltic coast into central Europe along a carefully selected route that
would ensure they lodged in friendly territory until they reached
their destination. Europe to Dee must have been a mental construct
mapped along religious boundaries, with criteria of accessibility
that were unique to his age.

Also unique to his age, but coming from a very different starting
point, is a map of Europe held in the Strahov Library in Prague,
which is a symbolic representation of *Europa* as a virgin, dated
1592. The virgin's head, wearing a crown, is Hispania, her shoulders
Gallia, her left arm curves round the Dutch coast, bending at the
elbow into Dania, and her fingers grip a slender rod which cuts off
Norvegia and Svetia. Her right arm stretches down through Italia,
and the orb she holds is Sicilia. The collar around her neck are the
Montes Piranei, the curve of her neckline contains Gallia, her breasts
are Germania and Swevia, with a glowing golden heart that is
Bohemia. Her long gown stretches out through Polonia as far as
Moscovia on the left hand side, and down through Albania and

Graecia to the Pelepponesus on the right. A great artery runs down her body, through the cities of Vienna, Buda and Alba Graeca into a delta at the hem of her skirt. Parallel to this artery runs a decorative border of mountains, from Illiricum to Constantinopolis. The entire gown from collar to hem is coloured green, making the uncoloured patches of the southernmost tip of Norvegia and Svetia, along with the northernmost part of Mauritania and the easterly part of Asia Minoris, stand out palely in comparison. Most significantly, the uncoloured islands of Anglia and Hiebernia float just beside her left ear, disproportionately large in relation to the rest of the map. The defeat of the Spanish Armada four years earlier in 1588 had effectively ended the Emperor's ambitions of annexing the islands, but the sheer size of these uncoloured land masses floating so tantalizingly close to the virgin's crown suggest that they remained an object of desire. This vision of Europe, which reflects the imperial concept of a continent united under the crown of imperial Spain is a map of the Europe that Dee fearfully avoided as he plotted his course through safe Lutheran and Calvinist lands, out of the emperor's range.

The unknown map-maker who produced that text may have been working on it at the same time that Fynes Moryson – a student of Peterhouse, Cambridge, as he describes himself in his opening sentence – set off on his journey round Europe that was published as *His ten Yeeres travels thorow Twelve Dominions*. The first of these journeys, in 1591, followed a similar route to that of Dee's party, but contains considerably more detail of what happened along the way. Fynes Moryson, appropriately for a student, is obsessively concerned with how much things cost, and recounts little anecdotes about people and places. His first account of Prague gives some indication of the tone of his writing:

So as Prage consists of three Cities, all compassed with wals, yet is nothing lesse than strong, and except the stinch of the streetes drive back the Turkes, or they meete them in open field, there is small hope in the fortifications thereof. The streets are filthy, there be divers large market places, the building of some houses is of free stone, but for the most part are of timber and clay and are built with little beauty or Art, the walles being all of whole trees as they come out of the wood, the which with the bark are laid so rudely, as they may on both sides be seen. Molda in the winter useth to be so frozen, as it beareth carts, and the ice thereof being cut in great peeces, is laid up in cellers for the Emperour and Princes to mingle with their wine in summer, which me thinkes can neither be savoury nor healthfull, since neither the heat of the clime, nor the strength of the Bohemian wines (being small and sharp) require any such cooling.[10]

With subsequent journeys, Fynes Moryson became increasingly confident, giving lengthy accounts of what people wore, the food they ate, their courtship and marriage practices, punishments and countless other details. He also began to address the reader directly and to offer advice to other travellers, assuming a far more authoritative role than the enthusiastic undergraduate voice of the first itinerary. And with the greater authority comes another more cautionary note: 'a traveller must sometimes hide his money, change his habit, dissemble his Country, and fairly conceal his Religion.' Though more cynically, he warns against the foolishness of being caught in the wrong place with the wrong religious credentials, and advises travellers to hold their tongues:

> Let them stay at home who are so zealous, as they will pull the Hostia or the Sacrament out of the Priest's hand. They should do better to avoid the adoring thereof, by slipping out of the way, or restraining their curious walkes, for inordinate desire of Martyrdome is not approvable.

Fynes Moryson and Dee both travelled across the body of Europa, but their accounts are different in tone, content and intent. Dee wanted to record his encounters with spirits, with the geographical data secondary, whilst Fynes Moryson recorded a random collection of anecdotes, experiences, vignettes and images. Reading Moryson's *Itineraries* we lose track of where he is, and although he tells us that it took him two and a half days to reach Augsburg from Nurenberg and his horse cost him two dollars, his concern is not with the spatial at all. Dee's account of his journey is conditioned by his experience as a map-maker, Fynes Moryson is out on a kind of quest, wandering through the world, in search of adventures. Significantly, he notes the size and strength of fortifications in the cities he visits, because a constant subtext in his writing is the fear of attack by the Turks. Most important of all, however, is the narrative persona, for whilst Dee's narrative is presented as a series of notes and jottings, Fynes Moryson's is a carefully crafted whole, with a dominant I speaker who leads the reader with him along the roads of Europe, pausing occasionally to preach, to patronize and to give advice to those he deems more inexperienced.

The debates on translation that have raged on down the centuries have frequently concerned the visibility or lack of it of the translator. Is the translator a transparent channel, a kind of glass tube through which the Source Language text is miraculously transformed in its passage into the Target Language, or is the translator herself an element in that process of transformation? Similar questions have begun to be asked about map-makers, questions that challenge the supposed objectivity of a map and ask what the map might be for, what might it be seeking to represent. Post-colonial theory has called into question the organization of geographical space, inviting us to consider the prioritizing of the starting point, the cultural base of the map-maker. So European Renaissance cartographers prioritize Europe, just as Piri Reis (c.1470–1554), the great Turkish mariner and author of the *Kitab-i-Bariye*, gave priority to the Muslim Mediterranean world.

The map-maker, the translator and the travel writer are not innocent producers of text. The works they create are part of a process of manipulation that shapes and conditions our attitudes to other cultures while purporting to be something else. Map-makers produce texts that can be used in very specific ways, translators intervene in the interlingual transfer with every word they choose, travel writers constantly position themselves in relation to their point of origin in a culture and the context they are describing.

In 1992, the *Independent* newspaper published a map of the new Europe to assist its readers in orienting themselves with the collapse of the communist regimes in the East. The opening of borders immediately called into question the very terminology that had been in place for decades. Finally, it could be recognized that Vienna is, in geographical terms, much further to the East than Prague, a city formerly designated as part of Eastern Europe. The language of East and West, borrowed from geography, had come to acquire a political significance, just as the language of North and South does in Ireland (the most northerly geographical point in Ireland is in the South, and Willie Docherty's captioned photograph, entitled *The Other Side* states that 'West is South' and 'East is North', an

apparent conundrum that is completely comprehensible to anyone familiar with the situation in Northern Ireland.[11] The 'North' or
that part of the island which is designated as part of the United
Kingdom does not contain the most northerly geographical point.
The northernmost tip of Ireland is therefore technically in the South,
i.e. in the Republic of Ireland.

The *Independent* map offers a new enlarged version of Europe.
This Europe does not stop at the Black Sea, the point generally
regarded as the most easterly boundary in the twentieth century.
Previous boundaries had been many and varied, depending on
political as well as on linguistic criteria. In 1834, Alexander Kinglake,
author of *Eothen, or Traces of Travel Brought Home from the
East*,[12] noted: 'I had come, as it were, to the end of this wheel-going
Europe, and now my eyes would see the splendour and havoc of the
East'. He had reached Belgrade. The new Europe stretches out round
the edges of the Black Sea, northwards through Georgia, south-
wards through Turkey, round and across to the Turkic republic
of Azerbaijan, right over to the Caspian Sea. Suddenly Europe
has stretched, changed direction, moved thousands of miles into
what was once Asia. What are we meant to read into this revision
of geographical, ethnic, religious and political boundaries? That
because the former Soviet union was classified as a European state,
now that it has ceased to exist its component parts are *de facto* part
of Europe too? (though not all the component parts, by any means).
That the map-makers see the conferral of European status as a
positive attribute? That EEC states are looking hungrily towards the
natural resources said to lie beneath the soil of what were once
termed Central Asian states? That we should all now wipe out
centuries of conditioning that saw Islam, as Edward Said puts it, as
symbolic of 'terror, devastation, the demonic, hordes of hated
barbarians'.[13]

Besides, the *Independent* map-maker was so concerned with
looking out to the Caspian Sea that Iceland has been cut off
altogether. The small, Scandinavian island up in the North Atlantic
has suddenly, like Atlantis, vanished without trace. Could such an
omission have anything to do with the end of the Cold War, we may
ask, and with the abrupt demise of Iceland's importance as a
strategic base for the monitoring of Soviet military action? The
omission was not remedied in the enlarged version of the map which
followed the first one. One stroke of the pen added Azerbaijan and

subtracted Iceland from what is now a Europe that stretches across a continent and a half. Only the southern parts of Norway, Sweden and Finland appear. The whole bias of the map is away from Northern Europe towards those areas that were once part of the Roman Empire: Bithynia and Pontus, Cappadocia, Armenia, Colchis and the Caucasus. The rise and fall of the Ottoman Empire is wiped away with this cartographical manipulation.

In Fynes Moryson's Europe, the fear was of encroachment by the Turks, and during the reign of Suleiman the Magnificent (1520–1655) the Ottoman empire had extended down as far as the Persian Gulf and northwards through what is now part of the Ukraine, northwestwards through part of Hungary, Croatia and Slovenia. Unable to capture Vienna in 1529, there was to be a second Turkish siege of the city as late as 1689, and in the latter half of the seventeenth century the Ottoman empire claimed a large part of what is now southern Poland, territories in the Caucasus, Cyprus and Crete. Fynes Moryson's anxiety was based on concrete evidence: the Ottoman military machine was highly efficient, the annexation of lands systematic and thorough.

So if we want to try to imagine how Dee or Moryson constructed a mental map of the world, we have to think of 1) a Europe divided and mapped out according to religious frontiers; 2) a Europe, Catholic and Protestant alike, looking nervously eastwards scanning the horizon, like the soldiers at the outpost in Dino Buzzati's wonderful novel, *Il deserto dei Tartari*, for possible signs of movement that could signify attack; and 3) a Europe reaching greedily out across the Atlantic, seizing the opportunity to penetrate and fertilize virgin lands.

It is incontestable that the discourse of the great age of colonialization makes extensive use of gender metaphors. 'Oh my America', says John Donne of his Mistress's naked body: 'my new found land'. And a growing body of scholarship suggests that this figurative language extends a long way back, through medieval Europe into Roman times. Outside the boundaries of what a culture deemed to be 'civilization', all kinds of terrors lurked, and those terrors were frequently depicted in terms of sexual difference. New territories could therefore be described as 'virgin' lands; the notion of a rich Orient was linked to eroticism and lasciviousness ('the beds i' the East are soft', says Shakespeare's Anthony (*Anthony and Cleopatra*, II.iii.50); and fantasizing about the sexual habits of other cultures led (as it still does in a great deal of contemporary travel writing) to unsubstantiated generalizations of the kind proclaimed by Tacitus when he announced:

> Thus it is that the German women live in a chastity that is impregnable, uncorrupted by the temptations of public shows or the excitements of banquets. Clandestine love affairs are unknown to men and women alike . . . The young men are slow to mate, and their powers, therefore, are never exhausted.[14]

Tacitus is here describing the barbarians of the Northern forests, but from the perspective of a writer who argues that his own society has degenerated, while the Germans are still relatively unspoiled. Hence it was essential to present the Germans in idealized terms, in order for the corruption of the Roman world to be more sharply exposed.

Significantly, Tacitus was reread during the Reformation from a quite different perspective again: his account of the chastity of German women and the inherent nobility of German men could be cited as an example of the purity of the Protestant heritage in contrast with the excessive sensuality of Rome. Later still, as Ernest Renan has suggested, the distinction made by Tacitus between North and South, between Germans and Romans, was used in the struggle against Napoleon.[15] And, of course, Madame de Staël enshrined that binary opposition of north and south in her *De l'Allemagne* (1810).

In the age of imperial expansion of the nineteenth century, the split between north and south widened yet again. With the Ottoman Empire crumbling, the threat from the East diminished, and the tone of many writers introducing the East to fellow Europeans was distinctly patronizing and pejorative. Moreover, the tendency to describe alternative cultures in sexually figurative language took on another dimension. E. W. Lane, translator of the Arabian Nights (his version appeared in 1840) announced with a confidence reminiscent of Tacitus's assertions about the chaste Germans that:

> the women of Egypt have the character of being the most licentious in their feelings of all females who lay any claim to be considered as members of a civilized nation. . . . What liberty they have, many of them, it is said abuse; and most of them are not considered safe unless under lock and key . . . some of the stories of the intrigues of women in The Thousand and One Nights present faithful pictures of occurrences not infrequent in the modern metropolis of Egypt.[16]

Faithful pictures: the discourse of faithfulness that has so dogged translation studies and from which we are finally beginning to emerge is also a dominant discourse in travel writing. Travellers have pretensions towards faithfulness, insisting that we believe their accounts simply because they have been there and we have not. So Lane can assure us with confidence that Egyptian women are the worst in the world, while his contemporary, Richard Burton, provides us with the important information that tallow candles were forbidden in Harems and 'bananas when detected are cut into four so as to be useless'.[17] The line between pornography and travel writing is pretty finely drawn in certain cases.

Rana Kabbani and a range of other scholars drawing upon feminist methodologies have started to examine the way in which European travellers eroticize the Orient and transform it into the locus of their own sexual fantasies.[18] This is another whole new dimension of comparative literary studies and an important one, for as we learn how cultures construct other cultures, how the explicit and the implicit are woven together, so we also learn about the manipulative processes that underlie such self-proclaimed 'objective' or 'faithful' depictions of reality.

At the two poles of the *Independent* map of Europe is the vanished island of Iceland in the North Atlantic and the huge expanding Turkik realms in Asia. It says a great deal about how we structure our world that we have come to want our maps to be constructed along latitudinal and longitudinal lines, which leads inevitably to oppositions at different edges. A glance at alternative mapping conventions, such as the Mappa Mundi (c. 1290) shows what happens to a mental concept of the world when such linear conventions are not used: the top of the world is not the north but the East, where the sun (God) rises in glory and the centre of the earth, as Dante tells us in his *Divine Comedy*, is Jerusalem. With these conventions in place, the world is drawn quite differently, though it is worth noting that the designer of the Mappa Mundi did not forget to include the island of Ultima Thule, generally held to be Iceland, and put in the Orkneys and Faroe Islands as well. The oceans flow round the rim of the circular world, not as an expanse of uncharted water but as a gently encircling band.

The presence of the dog-headed beings, bat-eared humans, mermaids and griffins depicted in the Mappa Mundi have long since been dismissed by more 'rational, scientific' ages. Today, we want accuracy from our maps, we want to believe in the truth of maps, the lack of bias of map-makers. But the *Independent* map of Europe in the 1990s shows up the fallacy of that belief in objectivity, for in our acceptance of mapping conventions of whatever period, we consign our belief into the hands of the map-maker, just as when we read a translation we want to trust the good faith of the translator. And, as has already been pointed out, the activities of map-making, translating and writing about one's travels are never totally innocent activities.

Claudio Magris' book on the Danube (*Danubio*, 1986) explores the history of the binary opposition of north and south in European cultural history through a journey down the Danube, the river that flows out of the heart of Europe towards the east. Starting with the source of the Danube, which is also virtually the same as that of the Rhine, he looks in both directions, contrasting the symbolic significance of the two great rivers:

> Ever since the *Song of the Niebelungs* the Rhine and the Danube have confronted and challenged each other. The Rhine is Siegfried, symbol of Germanic virtues and purity, the loyalty of the Niebelungs, chivalric heroism, dauntless love of the destiny of the Germanic soul. The Danube is Pannonia, the kingdom of Attila, the eastern, Asiatic tide which at the end of the *Song of Niebelungs* overwhelms Germanic values: when the Burgundians cross it on their way to the treacherous Hunnish court, their fate – a Germanic fate – is sealed.[19]

The Song of the Niebelungs, which most contemporary Europeans know only through Wagner, is part of the body of Germanic epic poetry that reached its highest point in the Norse sagas of medieval Iceland. Significantly, and very significantly indeed if we consider the marginal position of Iceland today in topographical terms and in terms of European cultural history, the great Norse sagas remained outside the mainstream of medieval Europe. The sagas are the great European absent texts, a central part of contemporary Icelandic culture but largely unknown anywhere else. Had they been known, they might have changed the history of European literary production. Because they are relatively unknown, they offer instead the fascination of what might have been, texts that are to Iceland what the works of Hesiod and Homer are to Greece, as the preface to W. H. Auden and Paul Taylor's *Norse Poems* attests.

In 1871 William Morris made his first journey to Iceland, and the journals of his travels in 1871 and again in 1873 give an account of his attempts to engage with the unknown. After his return from the second journey he writes:

> The journey has deepened the impression I had of Iceland and increased my love for it. The glorious simplicity of the terrible and tragic, but beautiful land, with its well-remembered stories of brave men, killed all querulous feeling in me, and has made all the dear faces of wife and children and love and friends dearer than ever to me. I feel as if a definite space of my life had passed away now that I have seen Iceland for the last time . . . it was no ideal whim that drew me there, but a true instinct for what I needed.[20]

Morris' *Icelandic Journals* are curious texts. He gives meticulous details of where he went, together with maps, but they are quite remarkably unemotional. The impression on reading them is of a conscious attempt at self-restraint, as the following demonstrates:

> we all drove together up a steepish hillside on the top of which lay a comfortable-looking stead and a church bigger than usual, which was Ingialdsholl, the scene of the (fictitious) Viglundar saga. The folk were abed when we came, but they all tumbled out in the greatest good-temper when we knocked them up: then as the night was now well on, and gotten windy too, we asked leave to sleep in the church, in which all things were soon arranged while I sat by the kitchen fire to make cocoa and milk hot, all the household assisting . . . so to bed on the tombstones of Icelanders dead a hundred and fifty years, within the screen much and prettily carved: the stones were hard, and there was a goodish draught through the church floor, but all that made little difference to me five minutes after I had settled my blankets.

His daughter, who edited the journals, provides an explanatory footnote to this episode by his companion Eirikr Magnusson:

> Here Morris omits mentioning an incident unique in this journey. When he was 'settled in his blankets', he offered to tell us the Saga of Biorn, the Champion of the men of Hitdale. The offer was accepted readily enough; and he told the whole saga in abridgement with remarkably few slips, winding up with the old rhyme:

And here the saga comes to an end:
May all who heard, to the good God wend.
And the audience was still awake when he finished![21]

We look in vain for anything other than pedantically recorded
details of landscape, food and accommodation. Yet the Icelandic
journeys changed Morris as a writer. In 1876 he published his
versions of *The Story of Sigurd the Volsung and the Fall of the
Niblungs*, and a reading of his novels shows the way in which he
transformed the Icelandic landscape into the setting for his fantasy-
world fiction. Morris is an example of what can be termed the
'idealistic traveller', the utopian socialist aesthete who had already
created an Iceland of the imagination that he went in homage to visit.
Iceland was part of Morris' dream of a common northern inheritance, offering a model of democratic society and artistic richness.
    It was also the place where he could live out his fantasy of ideal
masculinity, the place where he could test himself against the
elements, push himself to the limits and suffer extremes of cold and
physical hardships with good English stoicism. His writing, under-
stated as it is, reflects that impulse. The Icelandic journals are terse
accounts of a nineteenth-century Englishman's journey of self-
discovery, even though presented as accounts of an actual journey
retracing the steps of heroes from the sagas. The absence of passion
in the journals becomes all the more interesting if we compare them
to Morris' unpublished and unfinished novel begun early in 1872
after his return from Iceland, edited a century later by Penelope
Fitzgerald, who named it *The Novel on Blue Paper*.[22] This intensely
autobiographical novel, an account of the love of two men for
one woman, reflects the crisis in Morris' own life, as he learned of
his wife's affaire with Dante Gabriel Rossetti. The manuscript ends
with John, Morris' alter-ego character, leaving his village and the
woman he loves to his rival, his brother Arthur, and setting off on
a journey. The bleakness of the Icelandic landscape and his recollec-
tions of the sufferings endured by ancient heroes seem to have
offered Morris an escape from his own suppressed grief and anger,
exacerbated no doubt by the fact that in June 1871 he had entered
into joint tenancy of his beloved Kelmscott Manor with none other
than Rossetti. The character of John, described as big, strong and
very masculine, contrasts with the character of Arthur (Rossetti),
who is sickly and studious. After kissing Clara, Arthur's lips 'were

trembling still with the sweetness of that very unbrotherlike kiss', while John whistles 'in sturdy resolution to keep his heart up'.[23] Wounded as he was emotionally, Morris must have sought consolation in a physical landscape that brought him face to face with the hardship suffered by men in other times. If Rossetti, with his Italian background, exemplified the sensuality of the South, Morris sought his own spiritual homeland in the warrior North.

The equation of Iceland with ideals of masculinity and northerness reached its apotheosis in the 1930s, when regular visitors from Hitler's Germany made pilgrimages to Iceland in order to observe at first hand ideal specimens of the Aryan race. W. H. Auden and Louis MacNeice, who travelled to Iceland for very different reasons, expose the consequences of holding up an imaginary ideal of Nordic purity. In their *Letters from Iceland* (1937), there is an outspoken rejection of the values of the society of the sagas, the world of male bonding and militarism that had earlier appealed to Morris:

> Great excitement here because Goering's brother and a party are expected this evening. Rosenberg is coming too. The Nazis have a theory that Iceland is the cradle of Germanic culture. Well, if they want a community like that of the sagas, they are welcome to it. I love the sagas, but what a rotten society they describe, a society with only the gangster virtues.[24]

Louis MacNeice's *Epilogue from Iceland* draws a picture of a society in decline, sold out by international capitalism:

> Us too they sold
> The women and the men with many sheep.
> Graft and aggression, legal prevarication
> drove out the best of us . . .
> And through the sweat and blood of thralls and hacks,
> Cheating the poor men of their share of drift
> The whale on Kaldbak in the starving winter.
> And so today at Grimsby men whose lives
> Are warped in Atlantic trawlers load and unload
> The shining tons of fish to keep the lords
> Of the Market happy with cigars and cars.[25]

For Morris and for Auden Iceland was inspirational. Both translated Norse poetry, both saw in the early model of democracy a socialist ideal, both saw similarities between their vision of Iceland and ancient Greece. Their Icelands were male societies, and on some level they play at being Vikings themselves, distanced from home and family, and though Auden is more playful than Morris (his *Letters to Lord Byron* are very funny), they are both part of the same game. Auden is at pains to dissociate himself from the Nazi view of Iceland as a place of racial purity, the repository of Aryan civilization, but nevertheless both the views of Iceland and its history come from the same source: from readings of Tacitus.

Travellers to Iceland stress the remoteness of the place, the virtues of human courage in surviving the harsh climatic conditions, the power of the great unknown texts of European cultural history. Generalizing, we can say that there is a tendency to perceive Iceland as a model of a fictitious Germanic past, and travellers such as Morris and Auden approached it with reverence. Grey, strong, terrible, bitter cold, solemn – these adjectives recur through Morris' *Journals*, and despite the greater levity of Auden's and McNeice's *Letters from Iceland*, the same notes prevail.

If the volcanic ruggedness of Iceland is seen as symbolic of the virtues of restraint and self-discipline, the beauties of Turkey and especially of Istanbul are repeatedly seen in terms of sensuality. Travellers' tales of sexual encounters with veiled ladies abound. Here is Alexander Kinglake's story of one such meeting in the streets of Constantinople:

Of her very self you see nothing, except the dark, luminous eyes that stare against your face, and the tips of the painted fingers depending like rosebuds from out of the blank bastions of the fortress. She turns, and turns again, and carefully glances around her on all sides, to see that she is safe from the eyes of Mussulman, and then suddenly withdrawing the yashmak, she shines upon your heart and soul with all the pomp and might of her beauty. And this, it is not the light, changeful grace that leaves you to doubt whether you have fallen in love with a body, or only a soul; it is the beauty that dwells secure in the perfectness of hard, downright outlines, and in the glow of generous colour. There is fire, though, too – high courage, and fire enough in the untamed mind, or spirit, or whatever it is which drives the breath of pride through those scarcely parted lips.[26]

There is a postscript to Kinglake's tale – the lady touches him and cries: 'There is a present of the plague for you', which he explains is a common Turkish joke against Christians. It is an odd story, which combines elements of voyeurism and sexual fantasy (the mysterious veiled lady exposing herself to a passing European) but without a sexual finale and stylistically it stands out from the surrounding narrative, being written in the present tense and the whole sequence starting with the tentative phrase 'And perhaps as you make your difficult way through a steep and narrow alley . . .' It also contrasts sharply with Kinglake's insistence on writing honestly ('my excuse for the book is its truth').

An earlier visitor to Turkey also insisted that she was telling the truth about the society she encountered. Lady Mary Wortley Montagu's Turkish letters describe the social customs, dress and conversations of aristocratic Turkish women she met during her stay in Constantinople. Lady Mary's letters are interesting in that she is concerned with dispelling fantasies about Ottoman sexual customs, as demonstrated by the letter of 10 March 1718 to her sister, describing a meeting with the favourite wife of the late Emperor Mustapha:

> I did not omit this opportunity of learning all that I possibly could of the Seraglio, which is so entirely unknown amongst us. She assured me that the story of the Sultan's throwing a handkerchief is altogether fabulous.[27]

The reference here is to a story by Paul Rycaut, recounted in his *Present State of the Ottoman Empire* (1668), which claims that 'the Damsels being ranged in order by the Mother of the Maids, he (the Sultan) throws his handkerchief to her, where his eye and fantasy best directs, it being a token of her election to his bed.'[28] Lady Mary cuts through the pornographic fantasies of the lascivious life of ladies of the seraglio: she continually seeks to draw parallels between the Turkish court and the courts of London and Vienna. One of her longest accounts tells the story of the Spanish noble-woman to whom, as she delicately puts it, 'the same accident happened to her that happened to the fair Lucretia so many years before her, but she was too good a Christian to kill herself as that heathenish Roman did.'[29] Instead, the Spanish lady refuses the ransom money and the liberty offered by her Turkish lover, having 'very discreetly weighed the different treatment she was likely to find in her native country'. Balancing the fact that her Spanish relatives would 'certainly confine her to a nunnery for the rest of her days' while her 'Infidel lover was very handsome, very tender, fond of her and lavished at her feet all Turkish magnificence' the Lady chooses a Muslim husband and rejects the offer of freedom from her Christian relations. The story is told with considerable glee, and Lady Mary obviously celebrates the unorthodox decision of the Spanish woman to choose her own way in life. In many respects Lady Mary's letters are a refreshing change from the conventions of voyeuristic 'truth-telling': they celebrate the rights of women to assert themselves, besides rejoicing in the opportunity to contradict male stereotypes of the Orient. It would be far too simplistic to describe Lady Mary as a feminist, and yet there are ways in which her letters prefigure some of the concerns of feminism later in the eighteenth century. Likewise, Julia Pardoe's *The City of the Sultan and Domestic Manners of the Turks* (1837) and *The Beauties of the Bosphorus* (1839) show an author concerned with rubutting the growing volume of pornographic travel writing that offered 'expert' insights into the sexual mores of the Orient.

Edward Said has argued that since the eighteenth century Western writers have constructed the Orient as the Other:

> Everyone who writes about the orient must locate himself vis-à-vis the Orient; translated into his text, this location includes the kind of narrative voice he adopts, the type of structure he builds, the kind of images, themes, motifs that circulate in his text – all of which adds up to deliberate ways of addressing the reader, containing the Orient and finally representing it or speaking on its behalf.[30]

Said's pioneering work on Orientalism has opened up a whole new dimension of critical discourse, and many of his arguments, applied to a text like *Eothen*, for example, stand up well. But recently feminist critics have challenged Said's assertively male stance, and Sara Mills, while acknowledging the importance of Said's work, proposes a counter view. In her book on women travel writers, she points out that the work of women travel writers 'cannot be fitted neatly within the Orientalist framework', suggesting that it 'seems to constitute an alternative and undermining voice because of the conflicting discourses at work in their texts.'[31]

If we compare two nineteenth-century accounts of British impressions of Constantinople, it becomes apparent straight away that two very different discourses are being used. Julia Pardoe, who visited the city in 1835, describes Guiuk-Suy, a popular beauty spot along the Bosphorus:

> called by the Europeans the Asian Sweet Waters . . . to the circumstance of its being intersected by a pretty stream of fresh water, which, after flowing along under the shadows of tall and leafy trees, finally mingles its pigmy ripples with the swifter waves of the channel. The Anadoli Hissari, or Castle of Asia, stands upon its margin, and painfully recalls the mind to the darker and sterner realities of life. . . . All ranks alike frequent this sweet and balmy spot. The Sultanas move along in quiet stateliness over the greensward in their gilded arabas, drawn by oxen glittering with foil and covered with awnings of velvet, heavy with gold embroidery and fringes, the carriages of the Pashas' harems roll rapidly past, decorated with flashing draperies, the horses gaily caparisoned . . . while the wives of many of the Beys, the Effendis, and the Emirs leave their arabas, and seated on Persian carpets . . . amuse themselves for hours, the elder ladies with their pipes, and the younger ones with their hand-mirrors, greetings innumerable take place on all sides; and the itinerant confectioners and water-vendors reap a rich harvest.[32]

This description follows the pattern established by Lady Mary Wortley Montagu and, though full of signs reminding us of the 'foreignness' of the scene, with *arabas* and Persian carpets, Sultanas and Beys, water-vendors and ladies smoking pipes, nevertheless stresses the normalcy of this kind of public encounter. This is a place frequented by large crowds, and Julia Pardoe endeavours to convey a sense of the multifariousness of those crowds, along with the general air of goodwill and community spirit. It is a very far cry from Alexander Kinglake's account of the Bosphorus, written at approximately the same time. Julia Pardoe portrays the Bosphorus as a stretch of glittering water, with the tree-lined grass verge so lovely 'that a visitor . . . might fancy himself in Arcadia'. Kinglake writes about 'the fathomless Bosphorus' and compares Constantinople to Venice:

> Venice strains out from the steadfast land, and in old times would send forth the Chief of State to woo and wed the reluctant sea; but

the stormy bride of the Doge is the bowing slave of the Sultan – she comes to his feet with the treasures of the world – she bears him from palace to palace – by some unfailing witchcraft, she entices the breezes to follow her, and fan the pale cheek of her lord – she lifts his armed navies to the very gate of his garden – she watches the walls of his Serail – she stifles the intrigues of his Ministers – she quiets the scandals of his Court – she extinguishes his rivals and hushes his naughty wives all one by one. So vast are the wonders of the Deep![33]

In Kinglake's account, the very waters that border Constantinople are sexualized. The sea at Constantinople is depicted as that favourite figure of nineteenth-century male pornographic fantasy, the all-capable beloved slave woman, who serves and services her master absolutely. *The Lustful Turk* had appeared in 1828, and similar novels were published throughout the century, featuring either the ravishing of European women by lascivious Orientals or the extraordinary sexual techniques of Oriental women as experienced by European men. A common feature of both these themes was the physical abasement of the woman, and her resultant enjoyment of the pleasures of whipping, rape and bondage. Kinglake's description of the Bosphorus reflects that kind of fantasy. Julia Pardoe gives us a fairly straightforward narrative account of groups of women meeting at a local beauty spot. Sara Mills' argument is that this kind of writing is typical of many women travellers, since women writers 'knew their accounts would be considered odd and eccentric, and would be accused of falsehood'.[34] Because their readers would tend to disbelieve accounts written by women, women travel writers took pains to describe scenes realistically, often supplementing their accounts with sketches. Kinglake, on the other hand, was in no doubt that his book on his travels to the Orient would appeal to readers, hence the jocularity of his style and his willingness to slide into fantasy, apparently without regard for the contradiction this posed to his insistence on the truthfulness of his account. Kinglake expected to be believed, and his fantasies about veiled beauties in the back streets of Constantinople matched the preconceptions of his readers. Julia Pardoe, in common with many other women travel writers, had no such expectations, and so stressed the ordinariness of life in the Orient, comparing rather than contrasting the life style of women in her own culture and in Turkey. It is also worth noting that women travellers in Turkey and other Oriental lands had access to the closed rooms that provided the locus of sexual fantasy for the European men excluded from them, and so their accounts derive from first hand experience, rather than from imagined impressions of harem life. This is particularly ironic if we consider the different attitudes to truthfulness of male and female travel writers in the eighteenth and nineteenth centuries. Sara Mills reminds us that it is essential to consider the texts within the discursive frameworks that produced them:

> It is important to consider both the production and reception of texts, since the way we read is largely a product of discursive frameworks. The division male/female is obviously not a satisfactory way of describing differences between texts, as many women write within the same discursive frameworks as men; however, the differences may be the result of judgements made about their texts rather than any intrinsic differences.[35]

The contrast between accounts of Constantinople written by Kinglake, who can be considered typical of a whole mode of seeing the Orient in terms of deviant sexuality, and the conscious efforts made by women writers to rebut male fantastic accounts of the same place, serve as a clear indication of the way in which writing about place is genderized. Likewise, the association of Iceland with fantasies of male stoicism and hardness reveal a similar process at work. Turkey and the Orient tend to be feminized, with all the value judgements associated with femininity, while Iceland and the far North tend to be depicted as the object of another kind of fantasy, the true site of perfect masculinity.

The tours of Iceland organized from Nazi Germany were based on that image, and tourists avidly photographed the tall, broad-shouldered blond supermen who typified a racial and sexual ideal. It is only relatively recently, as gender theory invites us to reconsider the sexuality of social structures and of image making, that there has been discussion of the homophilic aspects of the idealization of the male body in fascist iconography.

The *Independent* map of the new Europe of the 1990s represents yet another shift of perception. The virgin Europa, with the crown of Hispania on her head, stands above the lumpen mass of Asia Minoris, though travellers in the sixteenth and seventeenth centuries saw the threat from below as an ever-present menace. In the eighteenth and nineteenth centuries, as nationalist movements periodically redrew the map, the dichotomy between the civilized, masculine north and the passionate, feminine south (and east) became more marked. Utopian socialists like Morris, and later Auden and MacNeice, admired the north for its strength and solemnity, and although the latter disassociated themselves from the Nazi touring groups, they shared in different ways a fascination with the Nordic ideal.

Now, in the 1990s, comes another manifestation of the North/ South divide. The desire to appropriate areas that are commonly described as 'weak', 'underdeveloped', 'marginal' (and, though not explicitly stated but sharing the same vocabulary, 'feminine') in unclaimed areas of the world, lately around the Black Sea and the Caucasus, has led the map-maker to boldly assert the boundaries of Europe right into Asia. In contrast, a combination of contemporary political expediency (there are markets to be developed in the lands devolving out of the former Soviet Union) and a certain uneasiness with the former idealization of Nordic cultures has resulted in the elimination of Iceland from the new Europe. It would seem that the polarization of north and south, east and west is as strong as it has ever been, and is now beginning to be considered in terms of genderized language and the emerging history of colonial exploitation.

Map-making, travelling and translating are not transparent activities. They are very definitely located activities, with points of origin, points of departure and destinations. The great development in comparative literary studies is that such questions are now on our agenda. The time has come not only for us to compare accounts by travellers, but to question the premises on which those accounts were written in the first place. Like John Dee, we too are in the process of moving from simply mapping to the far more sophisticated science of balancing different systems of calculating times and dates.

6
Gender and Thematics:
the Case of Guinevere

Koelb and Noakes have suggested that in recent years there has been a shift away from the concerns of earlier comparatists, that is, away from the tendency to conceive of literary history as 'a great and unified cultural enterprise', away from the study of movements and themes.[1] They suggest, therefore, that there has been a move away from the proposition outlined by René Wellek in his essay determining the name and nature of comparative literature, in which he states that comparative literature 'is identical with the study of literature independent of linguistic, ethnic and political boundaries'.[2] Koelb and Noakes' collection of essays does indeed seek to move away from the 'universalization' approach, which perceives literature as an ennobling (and enabling) force for humankind that transcends all other barriers. The ideological implications of this attitude have already been discussed in previous chapters, for it assumes that there is such a thing as 'great' literature, and assumes also that whatever that thing is, it will unilaterally serve to 'raise' human beings who come into contact with it to some higher state. It also assumes that literary systems are somehow divorced from their contexts and can operate as free floating agents through time and space, across all forms of boundaries. It is, of course, a classic formalist viewpoint, and one which has been enormously influential in western Europe and in the United States.

However, in their eagerness to propose a comparative literature that is more in tune with world-wide literary trends at the end of the twentieth century, Koelb and Noakes have focused prominently on the growing relationship between literary theory and comparative study, which has inevitably led them to assume that the study of movements and themes has moved into the background. What this

chapter proposes, on the contrary, is that while they are quite right
to assume that there has been a move away from a concept of
comparative literature based on an assumption of a fundamentally
humanizing role of literature, there is another way of looking at
current trends in literary analysis. The study of themes and movements not only continues unabated, but possibly is even on the
increase. The difference is, of course, that the impulse is now coming from within areas of work defined under other headings than
that of 'comparative literature', such as post-colonial studies or
gender studies.

Siegbert Prawer devotes a whole chapter of his book on comparative literature to a discussion of what he calls 'themes and
prefigurations'.[3] He determines five different subjects of investigation, which include 1) the literary representation of natural phenom-
ena or what he calls 'perennial human problems and patterns of
behaviour'; 2) recurring motifs; 3) recurrent situations; 4) the
literary representation of types; 5) the literary representation of
named personages. He draws our attention to the fact that Raymond
Trousson has suggested that the most fruitful area for comparative
studies is the literary representation of named personages.[4] Prawer
insists, however, upon the significance of thematic study as a means
of showing not only how a theme might appear and disappear across
cultures as part of a study of literary history, but also as a means of
attempting to unravel why that process might have taken place. In
other words, the study of a theme 'should interest students of
literature no less than students of society and political ideas.'[5] In
her introduction to her anthology *The New Feminist Criticism*,
published in 1986, Elaine Showalter suggests that one of the earliest
manifestations of feminist criticism 'concentrated on exposing the
misogyny of literary practice: the stereotyped images of women in
literature as angels or monsters, the literary abuse or textual
harrassment of women in classic and popular male literature, and
the exclusion of women from literary history.[6] The second phase
of feminist criticism, according to Showalter, focused on texts
produced by women, with a view to revising traditionally male
determined literary history:

> so that we now have a coherent, if still incomplete, narrative of
> female literary history, which describes the evolutionary stages of
> women's writing during the last 250 years from imitation through

protest to self-definition, and defines and traces the connections throughout history and across national boundaries of the recurring images, themes, and plots that emerge from women's social, psychological and aesthetic experience in male-dominated cultures.[7]

Showalter's proposition is radical in that it forces a revision of assumptions about the literary canon, but it is surprisingly formalist and close to Wellek's view in its conception of movement across national boundaries. What she seems to be suggesting is that there is such a thing as universal patterning in the representation of women and in women's writing, regardless of the socio-economics and political contexts in which those texts are produced.

But the purpose of this chapter is not to continue the well-established debate on the historicity or otherwise of some conceptions of women's textual production. Rather the purpose is to draw attention to the importance that thematic study still has for many critics today, though not necessarily described as such. It is also significant that a great many women writers and artists are concerned with exploring archetypes, and with rewriting the story of some of the most prominent archetypal figures in western cultural history. So, for example, Ariane Mnouchkine's 1992 version of the story of the house of Atreus, *Les Atrides*, presents a sympathetic view of Clytemnestra as a woman betrayed by her husband Agammemnon into handing over her beloved daughter Ephigenia, supposedly to be married but actually to be sacrificed at her own father's hands. The image of Clytemnestra as an adultress, as the unfaithful wife who murders her husband on his return from Troy, thus appears in a very different light.

Equally, the remarkable interest in Medea by theatre companies right across Europe in the 1980s and 1990s reflects an attempt to come to terms with an archetype that has traditionally been seen as a figure of horror, the mother who murders her children. Interpretations of Medea vary from depicting her as an outsider, often a black woman, ostracized by Hellenic culture and considered dispensable when Jason needs to marry for political reasons, to depicting her as a loving wife and mother driven to desperation by an unfaithful, unloving husband. Yet other interpretations explore some of the issues raised by Adrienne Rich in her ground breaking book *Of Women Born: Motherhood as Experience and Institution* (1976) which examines the social implications of infanticide, and draws attention to evidence which suggests that infanticide was the most common crime in Western Europe for centuries.[8]

Reconsideration and re-evaluation of female archetypes from the Hellenic tradition, from Christian tradition (Mary Magdalene, the Virgin Mary etc.) from folktales and from fairy tales is more noticeably part of feminist artistic practice than part of feminist critical practice, where emphasis has tended to be placed on literary archetypes and Prawer's 'named personages'.

Sifting through the quantities of creative and scholarly work by women on figures from post-sixteenth-century literary history, from ancient mythologies, from folklore and fairy tale and from the Judaeo-Christian tradition generally, it is interesting to observe an apparent lack of interest in the tradition of Arthurian literature. Of course interest in Arthurian romance is still so strong generally in the Anglo-Saxon world that there are continuous reprints of established texts, rewritings in novel and cinematic form of various episodes relating to the Arthurian materials, international societies, journals and conventions devoted to studying the history and development of those materials. But the complex ambiguous figures of characters such as Morgawse, Nimue, Iseult or Guinevere have not yet received as much attention from feminist writers or critics as characters such as Jane Eyre, Electra, Judith or Salome, a significant absence given the way in which writers from different periods have portrayed such figures.

Margawse, Nimue (otherwise known as Nimiane or Viviane), Iseult and Guinevere recur in different ways, though generally treated as negative archetypes. Margawse, Queen of the Orkneys, is a half-sister of Arthur, and in Mallory's version, among others, is depicted as having had an incestuous relationship with her brother, resulting in the birth of Mordred, the man who will eventually bring about the ruin of the ideals of the Round Table. Like Clytemnestra, she is killed by one of her own sons who finds her guilty of adultery. She is often depicted as a sorceress, and in some of the twentieth-century novel versions of the Arthurian material she epitomizes evil; she is the Queen of Air and Darkness in T. H. White's *The Once and Future King*, a beautiful witch in contact with the powers of the dark in Gillian Bradshaw's *Down the Long Wind* trilogy.[9]

Nimue is also a sorceress, and like Margawse schemes to bring about the downfall of the forces of goodness. Nimue causes Merlin, Arthur's faithful magician, to fall in love with her, and when she has extracted from him secrets of his magic, she uses that magic to imprison him. Tennyson, who calls her Vivien, describes her as a kind of Lamia figure, a snake woman, 'a viper frozen' who seals the old man in a hollow tree forever, 'lost to life and use and name and fame.'[10]

Iseult and Guinevere come into a different category, that of unfaithful wives who are nevertheless faithful lovers until death. The treatment of Iseult has tended to be more consistent, perhaps because the story of the inadvertent beginning of the love between Iseult and Tristan, when they mistakenly drink the love potion intended for her new husband, creates an image of Iseult as innocent victim of passion. The treatment of the story of Guinevere, however, has been much more varied, and shifts in sympathy towards her on the part of different writers can arguably be said to reflect shifts in attitude towards the figure of a woman who seeks to determine her own destiny.

Norris J. Lacy and Geoffrey Ashe, who have compiled *The Arthurian Glossary*, refer to the Celtic, pre-Christian origins of much of the material, in particular in relation to the female characters:

> It has been suggested (as also, and more strongly in the case of Guinevere) that the romancers are dealing with traditions of Celtic queenship that, in the Middle Ages, are no longer comprehensible. A Celtic queen was her husband's equal, in some ways his superior, and could take lovers as a king could take concubines. Transplanted into the context of medieval wifely duty, the story becomes different and Iseult becomes theoretically 'bad'.[11]

The importance of the 'Mother Goddess' in ancient Irish culture is reflected in the *Song of Anergin*:

> I am the womb: of every holt,
> I am the blaze: on every hill,
> I am the queen: of every hive,
> I am the shield: for every head,
> I am the tomb: of every hope.[12]

The Mother Goddess, the Triple Goddess representing the cycle of birth, fecundity and death, had three manifestations: maiden, mother and crone or hag. These three symbolic archetypes recur throughout the Arthurian stories as different characters, but with the transformation into literary forms of a pre-Christian oral tradition, the power of the goddess had been significantly altered. Successive feminist studies of early matriarchal societies have shown how the shift to patriarchy was characterized by a radical change in the depiction of female deities. So from all-powerful goddess who controlled the passage into this world and out of it, we end up with a series of wicked witches, debauched queens, unstable wives and cruel lovers. Mary Condren has discussed the ways in which the relegation of the once powerful Irish goddess figures into a position of inferiority links up with the Judeao-Christian conception of woman as being responsible for the fall of Adam and of mankind.

The world of Arthurian romance emerged in a world of militarism, and the Round Table represents an ideal of knighthood. In such a society, as Condren points out, the Great Mother was marginalized:

> motherhood was no longer a source of strength but a handicap, preventing one sex from participation or representation in the prestigious culture of the warriors. . . . The Triple Goddess, whose spiral imagery represented life, death, and the cycle of eternal return, has been torn apart once and for all. The ambiguity and integration of the complex elements of matricentred religion, as represented by the Serpent/Goddess in the form of a Triple Spiral, would be overcome and replaced eventually by the Sign of the Cross . . . The Irish story has . . . preserved for us the true nature of the event: the matricide that lies at the heart of patriarchal culture and the Fall into patriarchal time and space that would have devastating consequences for the banished children of Eve.[13]

Like Greek mythology which charts another version of the transition from matriarchy to patriarchy, the destruction of the mother is a prominent motif. Clytemnestra and Margawse are depicted as dishonourable and dishonouring, and hence are killed by their own sons. Arthur is described constantly as the son of Uther Pendragon, the importance of his paternal lineage being supreme. As the great British hero, Arthur embodies all the virtues of military prowess, combined with good judgement, nobility and honesty. Except for one fatal flaw: his wife, Guinevere.

Geoffrey of Monmouth's *History of the Kings of Britain* (1136–8) contains an account of Arthur's betrayal by Guinevere. In

Geoffrey's version, she is described as having broken her marriage vows to live in adultery with Mordred, in this version Arthur's nephew, who had been left in charge of the kingdom while Arthur was absent fighting the Romans. Arthur returns, Mordred is defeated and Guinevere flees for her life to a convent. Arthur pursues Mordred and finally kills him, before he is himself mortally wounded. He is taken to the Isle of Avalon, and hands over his crown to his cousin Constantine, son of the Duke of Cornwall. The date, according to Geoffrey, was 542 AD.

The basic ingredients of Arthur as ideal ruler, but handicapped by an unfaithful wife, were therefore in place very early in the development of the Arthurian material. And with the shift from epic to romance, and the establishment of the conventions of courtly love, with its chaste idealization of the lady, there occurred a shift in treatment of the motif of Guinevere's infidelity. By the time Chrétien de Troyes came to write his romances, the significant alteration in the story is the addition of an ideal lover, the knight Sir Launcelot, hero of *Le Chevalier de la Charrette* (*The Knight of the Cart*) (c. 1179)

Chrétien depicts Launcelot in classic courtly mode as the true and faithful servant of his liege lady, Guinevere, who risks pain and humiliation to save her when she is abducted by the evil Meleagaunt. He also presents a sympathetic portrait of Arthur, who is never depicted as a cuckolded husband but always as the epitome of nobility and generosity. The tension present in this dual perspective creates split sympathies for a reader: on the one hand, the love between Launcelot and Guinevere is idealized and noble, on the other hand Arthur is the wronged husband whose loyalty to friend and to wife never falters. Chrétien's Guinevere is more a symbol than a character, the object of desire who is acted upon rather than acting.

The development of Guinevere as a lover caught in the dilemma of loving two equally noble men came gradually, though depictions of her were by no means consistent. It is noteable that Christine de Pizan does not include Guinevere in her *Book of the City of Ladies* (1405). Iseult is mentioned, as an example of a woman who loved too deeply and died for that love, but Guinevere is absent. Dante hints strongly at moral condemnation of Guinevere, when Francesca confesses that the beginning of her fatal affair with her brother-in-law Paolo began on the day that they both read Galeotto's account of the passion between Launcelot and Guinevere. For as the story of their love develops, so also does Guinevere come to assume greater significance in the account of the collapse of the Round Table.

The creation of a perfect knightly order is one of the fundamental components of the Arthurian material. Arthur, the divinely chosen ruler, creates a new order of knights, seated non-hierarchically around a circular table. From Arthur's hall the knights set out upon quests, performing prodigious military feats in the name of good-ness, and eventually, as the motif of the Holy Grail grew in importance, setting out in search of divine illumination. Only the most pure of all men is allowed a glimpse of the Holy Grail, and that emphasis on male purity tends to highlight the pervading presence of stories of female impurity. As worship of the idealized lady gave way to worship of a mysterious chalice containing the Blood of Christ, so the imperfections of the lady are highlighted. The theme of Guinevere's adultery takes on an altogether more sinister and important dimension, and she becomes the scapegoat and the symbol of the disintegration of the ideal male order of the Round Table. By failing to live up to the expectations of her lord, Arthur, Guinevere creates disaster for them both. The motif of doomed love that is pervasive in the Tristan and Iseult story is different in the versions of Launcelot and Guinevere, for while Iseult is depicted as never having loved anyone but Tristan, and therefore can be seen as a true lover despite her betrayal of her marriage vows, Guinevere is shown as a woman who starts well, as wife of the most noble king in Christendom, but who then falls into perdition through her inability to control her love for Launcelot. Guinevere is thus a dangerous emotive force in many of the romances, and becomes the symbol of disunity and disintegration. Like Eve, Guinevere is held responsible for the fall of man.

The popularity of the Arthurian material lasted for several centuries in the Middle Ages, and the Arthurian cycle, often termed the Matter of Britain, can fairly be said to rank alongside the other great European romance cycles, the Germanic cycles of the Nibelungenlied and the Norse sagas, the Matter of France, or accounts of the exploits of Charlemagne and his knights and the Matter of Rome, the accounts of the legends of Troy, of Alexander, of Aeneas. In the late fifteenth century, coinciding with the invention of printing, Sir Thomas Mallory produced his *Morte d'Arthur*, printed by Caxton in 1485, the year which also saw the beginning of the Tudor dynasty with the accession of Henry VII.

Mallory's epic draws upon a range of English and French versions, though he refers throughout, often with ironic humour, to the authority of 'the French book', which he insists is his source. His work gives an account of the accession of Arthur, the founding of the Round Table, the exploits of various knights, with particular emphasis on Tristan, Launcelot and Gawain. In Mallory's version the knight of the Holy Grail is Galahad, son of Launcelot and Elaine, who tricks him into believing that he is making love to his true lady, Guinevere. The passion between Launcelot and Guinevere is presented in matter of fact terms at the beginning of Book VI:

> he [Sir Launcelot] is the first knight that the French book maketh mention of after King Arthur came from Rome. Wherefore Queen Guinever had him in great favour above all knights, and in certain he loved the queen again above all other ladies damosels of his life, and for her he did many deeds of arms, and saved her from the fire through his noble chivalry.[14]

Mallory's Guinevere is an active character, imperiously ordering Elaine to leave Launcelot alone in a scene of rivalry that has become a staple of contemporary soap opera, and sending the errant Sir Pedivere on a pilgrimage to Rome to seek penance for having beheaded his wife when she had placed herself under Launcelot's protection. Mallory's world is a violent one, and although damsels in distress are often saved, they are also subjected to rape and other forms of violence. The context in which Mallory wrote was that of the Wars of the Roses, and his own violent story led to him being imprisoned for armed assault, banditry and rape. Mallory drew upon romance material produced under the ethos of the courtly love convention, but his treatment of that material shows him to be a man of a very different age. Significantly, his Guinevere is not condemned as an adultress, but presented as an example of true love:

> But nowadays men cannot love seven nights but they must have all their desires: that love may not endure by reason; for where they be soon accorded and hasty, heat so cooleth . . . Wherefore I liken love nowadays unto summer and winter; for like as the one is hot and the other cold, so fareth love nowadays; therefore all ye that be lovers call unto your remembrance the month of May, like as did Queen Guenever, for whom I make here a little mention, that while she lived she was a true lover, and therefore she had a good end.[15]

Mallory's account of the plot against Launcelot and Guinevere, of his being found in her chamber and Arthur being forced against his will to condemn her to death has provided the basis of most of the twentieth-century fiction versions. Arthur is reluctant to act, but is forced to do so by some of his knights, notably the sons of Margawse. Mallory draws upon his French 'source', but depicts Arthur's dilemma in few words: 'For as the French book saith, the king was full loth thereto, that any noise should be upon Sir Launcelot and his queen; for the king had a deeming, but he would not hear of it, for Launcelot had done so much for him and the queen so many times, that wit ye well the king loved him passingly well.'[16]

T. H. White develops the character of Arthur outlined by Mallory, offering us the portrait of a good man caught in the tragic reality of his wife's love for his best friend. Using the language of popular romantic fiction, White depicts Arthur's 'deeming' through a banal conversation charged with hidden meanings:

> Launcelot began to laugh, and the last strand of tension seemed to have broken.
> 'Would you,' he asked, 'marry a woman who chased you with a hatchet?'
> The King considered the matter gravely before he answered.
> 'I couldn't do that,' he said in the end, 'because I am married already.'
> 'To Gwen,' said Launcelot.
> It was peculiar. They seemed to have started talking with meanings which were separate from the words they used. It was like ants talking with their antennae.
> 'To Queen Guenever,' said the King, in contradiction.
> 'Or Jenny?' suggested the Queen.
> 'Yes,' he agreed, but only after a long pause, 'or Jenny.'[17]

The use of nicknames in this exchange is fraught with significance. Guenevere is Arthur's Gwen, but she is Launcelot's Jenny, she exists for each of them in different ways and is named accordingly. When Launcelot uses Arthur's pet name, Gwen, Arthur corrects him and uses her full title. Guinevere immediately counters by referring to herself with the pet name used by Launcelot, and in this way the dynamics of the trio can be discerned quite clearly, with all three caught in the trap of passion and friendship, with conflicting loyalties.

Mallory's Arthur is shown as a fundamentally good man, who never loses his nobility, and in White's novel, which traces the story of Arthur from magical childhood to disillusioned old age, Arthur is also the centre of attention, the character who invites the reader's sympathy and approval. Nevertheless, Mallory's Arthur, like White's, is both an ideal monarch and a human being, and it is the relationship with his wife that provides the focus for developing the human dimension. Though both wrote against a background of war (the first three volumes of *The Once and Future King* came out in 1939, 1940 and 1941 respectively), the military prowess of Arthur is less significant than that of his knights, and it is Launcelot in both texts who is the questing hero, with Arthur more of a contemplative figure. The old king at the end of White's novel reflects on the destruction of the Round Table as the destruction of his belief in the perfectability of mankind:

> The service for which he had been destined had been against Force, the mental illness of humanity. His Table, his idea of Chivalry, his Holy Grail, his devotion to Justice . . . the whole structure depended on the first premise: that man was decent.
> Looking back at his life, it seemed to him that he had been struggling all the time to dam a flood . . . the flood of Force Majeure.[18]

White's Arthur, like Mallory's, comes to the end of his life as ruler of a waste land, the order of perfect knighthood destroyed, the love of his life and his best friend inadvertently responsible for the final battle. But significantly in both these versions, the blame for the final catastrophe is not placed on Guinevere. Rather, the story of the three lovers caught in a triangle of conflicting emotions and loyalties becomes a symbol of the disunion, and not the cause of it. And furthermore, Mallory and White stress the great sorrow at the heart of Arthur's marriage, the fact that Guinevere is childless.

The healing Grail, which can restore the dying to life, is no help to Arthur. Denied a child, and hence a succession, his kingdom disintegrates. It is, of course, notable that the issue of heirs who would ensure continuity and stability was of crucial importance in the fifteenth and sixteenth centuries. The death of Richard III in 1485 enabled the Tudors to take over the crown and, significantly, Henry VII named his first born son Arthur, in honour of the mythical king who, as Mallory relates 'shall come again and . . . shall win the holy cross.' The untimely death of Arthur meant that Henry VIII succeeded his father, and the problem of an heir remained high on the agenda throughout his reign and those of his three children: Edward VI, Mary and Elizabeth I.

In his book entitled *Learning to Curse: Essays in Early Modern Culture*, Stephen Greenblatt discusses the basic premises of 'new historicist' criticism. The new historicism, he suggests, involves looking at literary texts in such a way as to recover as far as possible the historical circumstances of their original production and reception, and then to analyse the relationship between those circumstances and the circumstances of the critic. New historicism is therefore a comparative methodology, only the process of comparison takes place across time boundaries rather than across geographic ones. White's detailed study of Mallory, as writer and as man, and his attempt at bridge building between the despair he experienced in the early years of the Second World War and the troubled violent world of the late fifteenth century is also an exercise in comparing. White, like the critics discussed by Greenblatt, also sought to understand 'the intersecting circumstances not as a stable, prefabricated background against which the literary texts can be placed, but as a dense network of evolving and often contradictory social forces.'[19]

Despite Henry VII's symbolic naming of his son, the rise of the English Renaissance marked the decline of the Arthurian material. Shakespeare, who took his plots from all kinds of sources, ignored Arthurian subjects, and Roger Ascham, the humanist scholar who taught the young Elizabeth I, dismissed Mallory's work in contemptuous terms:

> In our forefather's time, when Papistry, like a standing pool, covered and overflowed all England, few books were read in our tongue, saving certain books of chivalry, as they said for pastime and pleasure, which, as some say, were made in monasteries by idle monks, or wanton canons: as one, for example, *Morte Arthure*: the whole pleasure of which book stands in two special points, in open manslaughter and bold bawdiness: in which book those be counted the noblest knights that do kill most men without any quarrel and commit foulest adulteries by subtlest shifts: as Sir Launcelot with the wife of King Arthur his master: Sir Tristram with the wife of King Mark his uncle: Sir Lamerok with the wife of King Lot, that

was his own aunt. This is good stuff for wise men to laugh at, or honest men to take pleasure at. Yet I know when God's bible was banished the court and *Morte Arthure* received into the prince's chamber.[20]

Ascham's complaint about the immorality of the stories of Arthur and his knights reflects a common concern of liberal humanism, for the stable marriage mirrored the stability of the state. Catherine Belsey notes that

> early in the sixteenth century ... the circulation of humanist dis-courses in English produced new definitions of good government in the state and in the family. The humanist subject ... was to be per-suaded rather than coerced, and a sound (and persuasive) education was probably enough to guarantee a rational and virtuous adult.[21]

In such a context it is easy to see why the Arthurian material might be seen not only as unedifying, but also as dangerously immoral. Ascham does not discuss the establishing of a knightly order, or the quest for the Holy Grail, neither of which would have had much resonance in the new world order of the sixteenth century. Instead, he emphasizes the brutality and the sexual excesses of Mallory's characters, and above all the ever-present motif of adultery.

The Arthurian material declined to such a degree that it all but disappeared for centuries. Bits and pieces appeared in the late eighteenth century, but it was not until the mid-nineteenth century that writers and artists turned once again to the matter of Arthur for inspiration. What they did with it, and how they retold the story exposes some of the contradictions at the heart of Victorian society that critics have so frequently discussed – the contrast between images of idyllic childhood and the prevalence of child prostitution, the ideal of the 'Angel of the House' and the number of writers obsessed with woman's adultery, the discrepancy between the image of England as the powerhouse of the world and the appalling social conditions in which the workers who toiled in that powerhouse lived, the development of an ideal of Englishness set against a back-ground of xenophobia and overt racism.

Two texts in particular deserve consideration as examples of the tensions created by patterns of contradiction in how the Arthurian material is handled: Tennyson's *Idylls of the King*, and William Morris' *The Defence of Guinevere*.

Tennyson's poem, consisting of twelve books, was completed in 1869, though he had first started writing Arthurian poems in the 1830s. Mallory's *Morte d'Arthur* had been published again in 1816 and 1817, and was widely available. Tennyson bases much of his work on Mallory, but with significant differences. His Arthur is an ideal figure, but devoid of sensuality. The first book, entitled 'The Coming of Arthur', opens with four lines describing the beauty of Guinevere – 'she was fairest of all flesh on earth' – and her father's passionate love for his daughter.[22]

Subsequent books trace the slow decline of idealism, as Arthur is caught in the struggle between the fleshly and the spiritual. In 'Balin and Balan' (Book V), the Grail is first mentioned, and the knights set out 'To learn what Arthur meant by courtesy,/ Manhood, and knighthood.'

Straight after this revelation, Balin overhears Launcelot and Guinevere in the garden, and the seeds of doubt are sown. Sir Garlon suggests that Arthur's 'fair wife-worship cloaks a secret shame', the first overt hint of Guinevere's adultery, which is reinforced by the enchantress Vivien. The next book takes up the story of Vivien's destruction of Merlin, and the opening line is a dark premonition: 'A storm was coming, but the winds were still'.

The passion between Launcelot and Guinevere is seen at its most poignant in Book VII, 'Launcelot and Elaine'. As Elaine, Guinevere's 'guiltless rival', dies for love of the man who will not love her in return, her grieving father speaks the truth that has hitherto been suggested but not stated outright:

> This I know, for all the people know it,
> He loves the Queen, and in an open shame:
> And she returns his love in open shame;
> If this be high, what is it to be low?

The key motif of 'shame' returns finally in Book XI, 'Guinevere'. This penultimate book concentrates on Guinevere as fugitive, after she has fled to the convent, to escape from Madred and the ravages of war. Tennyson depicts a woman distraught with grief and guilt, refusing even to reveal her name. In a scene of classic Victorian melodrama, Guinevere talks to a young novice who gives her version of events at court, in which Guinevere is consistently described as 'the wicked queen', 'the woman whose disloyal life/ hath wrought confusion in the Table Round', 'the sinful queen'. Unable finally to control her temper, Guinevere sends the novice away, and then enjoys a brief period of reminiscence, during which Tennyson comes as close as he ever does to offering some insights into her character. She recalls the moment she first saw Arthur, as his bride:

> And moving through the past unconsciously,
> Came to that point where first she saw the King
> Ride toward her from the city, sigh'd to find
> Her journey done, glanced at him, thought him cold,
> High, self-contained, and passionless, not like him,
> 'Not like my Launcelot'

Her reverie is interrupted by the arrival of Arthur, who accuses her and forgives her in typical Victorian style,

> And while she grovell'd at his feet,
> She felt the King's breath wander o'er her neck,
> And in the darkness o'er her fallen head,
> Perceived the waving of his hands that blest.

Recognizing too late that it was her duty to love 'the highest', Guinevere commits what is left of her life to God and remains in the convent. The last book, 'The Passing of Arthur', returns to Mallory to recount the end of the hero king.

What makes Tennyson's portrayal of Guinevere so interesting are the tensions within it. She loves, and is punished for that love, but the terms in which her love for Launcelot are described rely on words such as error, sin or shame. This is not a noble or ennobling love, it is a secret, guilty love, and in her final confontation with Arthur, he is represented as a noble, forgiving man who can still admit that he loves her 'polluted flesh'. The tension derives from Tennyson's obvious fascination with Guinevere's physical beauty, with the way in which she reappears consistently throughout the twelve books as a figure of passion and of springtime, and with his attempts to exonerate her by depicting Arthur as cold in comparison with the loving Launcelot.

The dedication of the *Idylls of the King* is to the memory of Prince Albert, Queen Victoria's consort who had died in 1861. The author urges her not to grieve excessively, promising her the

prospect of heavenly reunion with her dead husband. Victoria is
certain of that reunion:

> May all love
> His love, unseen but felt, o'ershadow Thee,
> The love of all Thy sons encompass Thee,
> The love of all Thy daughters cherish Thee,
> The love of all Thy people comfort Thee,
> Till God's love set Thee at his side again!

Guinevere, however, is less certain, though Arthur holds out to her
the promise that if she purifies her soul and leans on Christ,

> Hereafter in that world where all are pure
> We two may meet before high God and thou
> Will spring to me, and claim me thine, and know
> I am thine husband – not a smaller soul,
> Nor Launcelot, nor another.

Tennyson's poem is a lament for the state of England, for the land
described in the final address to the Queen as 'some third-rate isle
half-lost among her seas'. The Arthurian material provides Tennyson
with a means to explore the state of his own age, as the explicit preface and postface demonstrate. Reading it today, however, what is
so striking is the ambiguous treatment of female sexuality. Guinevere
is passionate in contrast with Arthur's spiritual coldness, but she is
punished for being what she is stated to be from the outset. The
antithesis of duty, she defies the laws of 'ocean-empire with her
boundless homes/ Forever broadening England', and like the hun-
dreds of nameless women recorded in Françoise Barret-Ducrocq's
Love in the Time of Victoria, she is ultmately the loser.[23]

The *Defence of Guinevere and other poems*, (1858) was the first
volume of Pre-Raphaelite poetry to appear. In the same year Morris
painted his future wife, Jane Burden, as Guinevere, and the combination of painting, dramatic poem and choice of title for his
collection testify to his fascination for the figure of the mythical
queen. What fascinates Morris especially, however, is the queen's
sensuality. He paints Guinevere as fastening a belt around her
gown, apparently dressing, while a male figure in red plays the lute
in the rear of her chamber and she looks down at a dresser on which
there are two books. The central focus of the painting is the bed,

immediately behind her and filling most of the frame. It is wildly disordered, with sheets rumpled and the embroidered coverlet thrown back, and in the space vacated by whoever has occupied it, a small vulpine dog is curled up asleep. We are left in little doubt that Guinevere is dressing after a passionate encounter with a lover, and the brilliant sensual reds and oranges reinforce that impression. That Morris should have painted his wife in this role seems today curiously prophetic.

The long poem which gave the title to Morris' collection is written in *terza rima*, and is effectively a dramatic monologue. It takes up the moment of Guinevere's trial, and endeavours to construct an argument in her defence. Like Tennyson's *Idylls*, the first image we have is of Guinevere, but in Morris' version she is a creature under pressure, almost hunted:

> But, knowing now that they would have her speak,
> She threw her wet hair backward from her brow,
> Her hand close to her mouth touching her cheek[24]

Guinevere's defence proceeds through several stages. She begins by offering an image of the final judgement, of a dying man having to make a choice and choosing wrongly. The implication is that she made the wrong choice, taking Arthur instead of Launcelot, and this is reinforced by the first use of the three line refrain beginning 'Nevertheless you, O Sir Gauwaine, lie'.

The second stage of her defence is where she recounts the joy she felt when Launcelot first came to Arthur's court, an event that shed new light on 'the time ere I was bought/ By Arthur's great name and his little love'. She suggests here that she was forced into marriage, and it is significant that whereas Arthur features prominently in Tennyson, he hardly appears at all in Morris' version. The second stage proceeds through her telling of the first kiss in the garden, a sequence based (perhaps unconsciously) on Dante's Paolo and Francesca episode in *Inferno* V. This explicit admitting of the sexual passion between them concludes with the refrain again, after which she changes direction.

Now she proceeds through a carefully reasoned argument constructed around stereotypes of female behaviour, starting with the adulterous queen who ignores her conscience and destroys those who know the truth about her. This, she claims, is what she would have done had she been truly guilty, and she deliberately addresses Gawain directly, appealing to his friendship and his pity, seeking to win him over by proving her basic goodness. She reminds him of the caring role she has always played at court, and comes at last to the evidence against her, the blood in her bed that came from Launcelot's wound. Her argument is succinct: there is no single explanation for the blood – 'is there any law/ To make a queen say why some spots of red/ Lie on her coverlet?'

Having raised the taboo possibility of menstruation, the ultimate female characteristic, Guinevere moves on to attack the male values and responses that led to the fight within her chamber and the death of her accuser, Mellyagraunce:

> For Mellyagraunce had fought against the Lord;
> Therefore, my lords, take heed lest you be blent
>
> With all this wickedness; say no rash word
> Against me, being so beautiful; my eyes
> Wept all away to grey, may bring some sword
>
> To drown you in your blood; see my breast rise,
> Like waves of purple sea, as here I stand . . .

This final appeal relies on a combination of threat (someone, that is Launcelot, will come and perhaps destroy them) and instinctive belief that her beauty will be strong enough to overcome them. 'Will you dare,' she asks, 'when you have looked a little on my brow/ To say this thing is vile?'

This is her last weapon; the movement of the poem changes again, and now Guinevere's tone becomes more uncertain. She contrasts her past happiness with Launcelot with her present loneliness, reliving the moment when he came to her and they were discovered together. For the third time she speaks the refrain, concluding with the line 'All I have said is truth, by Christ's dear tears', and the last lines of the poem are told in the third person, as Guinevere hears the sound of Launcelot riding in to save her.

'The Defence of Guinevere' is in many respects a typical Pre-Raphaelite work, conscious of its own medievalizing, aiming at arousing sensations and creating a rich picture of another age. It is also typical in dealing with the theme of the *femme fatale*, the woman whose beauty lures men to destruction and which was such a powerful image throughout the nineteenth century, as scholars such as Mario Praz have shown.[25]

William Morris and his fellow Pre-Raphaelites seem to have been fascinated by the idea of women who transgress. Although they depicted idealized images of women in their writing and their art, they also created a range of *femmes fatales* – Guinevere, Lilith, Helen of Troy and figures from Greek mythology such as Circe. Women are presented as powerful but dangerous, and the danger derives from their sexuality. Rossetti, more than Morris, portrayed prostitutes and 'fallen women', and that very Victorian terminology stands in contrast to the ideal image of woman as an angelic figure. Morris' poem is a good example of the ambiguity of Victorian male attitudes to women who seek out their own happiness, for though on the one hand Guinevere is shown as strong-willed and determined to rebut the charges against her, the case she presents is based on the power of her sexual attraction, on her womanliness presented in physical terms, and ultimately she does not succeed and has to be rescued. Her arguments are all emotional, and her physical expression of that emotion is highlighted throughout.

With Tennyson's portrayal the perspective changes; Guinevere is punished for daring to love, despite the coldness of her husband, because, as the final scene between her and Arthur shows, she has failed in her duty to serve the force of righteousness. There are obvious parallels between Tennyson's Guinevere and characters from nineteenth-century fiction, particularly some of Thomas Hardy's women, where the clash between desire and duty leads to catastrophe.

The nineteenth and twentieth centuries have seen a proliferation of works based on the Arthurian material, some of which have had huge international success. White's novel provided the basis for the musical *Camelot*, and for the film of that musical, as well as for the Disney film *The Sword in the Stone*. There have also been a number of versions for children and for teenagers, where the material is reshaped in accordance with the tastes of the target reading group. Gillian Bradshaw's *Down the Long Wind* trilogy, a version following conventions of the romantic novel, tells the story from different perspectives. Bradshaw follows the now traditional device of moving from springtime to winter, from signs of hope to signs of despair. The final volume, *In Winter's Shadow*, is told in the first person by Guinevere, here in the Welsh spelling Gwynhwfar.

Bradshaw's character has an unhappy family background, so that her marriage to Arthur is a welcome escape, and from the first chapter the fact of Gwynhwfar's childlessness is emphasized along with Arthur's loving refusal to divorce her in order to beget an heir. Bradshaw's version depicts a woman with great emotional needs who falls unexpectedly in love (in this version with Bedwyr). Although written in 1982 it relies on stereotypes of feminine behaviour that Tennyson would have recognized, though with some concessions to twentieth-century domestic melodrama conventions – the protagonist 'staggers' from rooms with 'trembling hands' and her husband the king is 'burdened with Empire' and so has little time for her. Bradshaw's version transforms the story of Guinevere, Arthur and Launcelot into a suburban drama. It is *Brief Encounter* taken several stages further and in fancy dress.

What can be gained from looking at texts across a wide time span that deal with the same basic material? This question has concerned generations of comparatists, and the crux of the debate between comparative study as literary history or as practical comparing of texts regardless of context can be seen in differing attitudes to the tracing of thematic material across cultural and temporal boundaries. Koelb and Noakes imply that thematic studies have had their day and in so far as formalist methods are concerned that is probably right. Noting similarities between unrelated texts is good pedagogic practice in the classroom and helps break down prejudices about the uniqueness of literary systems but the comparison of one text with another without contextual reference is a formalist exercise that rapidly becomes tedious.

Prawer attacks Croce for suggesting that there is no significant connection between characters of the same name in the work of different writers, and for arguing instead that it is the personality of the writer that is the main protagonist,[26] yet Croce's argument would find some sympathy in a post-modern context for he points out that it is the way in which an individual writer handles the material, as a product of a particular moment in time, and, as we would argue today, of a particular ideology, that conditions what happens to that material in terms of its presentation, its production, and its reception.

This brief sketch of interpretations of the figure of Guinevere revealsa great deal about changes in literary conventions and also about changes in ideology, particularly with regard to the sanctity of marriage and the expected role of the ideal wife. Whether or not we accept the assumption that the figure of Guinevere like that of Iseult, Margawse and other powerful enchantresses derives from debased images of Celtic goddesses, which seems a likely hypothesis, what is very clear is that the problem of dealing with her story does not diminish but rather increases the further we move away in time from those religious origins. The cult of courtly love provided a framework within which the story of a queen who chose love outside marriage could be told without blame, but the dominant Christian ideology of the age, that savagely crushed the Cathars and other similar sects, and founded the patriarchal university system that was to dominate thought for centuries to come, ensured that the story of Guinevere would be linked to the primal sin of that other fallen woman, Eve.

The resurgence of interest in the medieval world in the nineteenth-century (albeit a nineteenth century version of the Middle Ages) exposes a tension in the gap between the violence of the material and the expectations of readers, parallel to the gap between overt and covert images of sexuality of the time. Tennyson tackles the Arthurian subject matter, but constantly smoothes it out, softens it, so that Uther's rape of Arthur's mother Ygerne, for example, becomes

> Enforced she was to wed him in her tears,
> And with a shameful swiftness . . .

Dominant ideals of feminine behaviour conditioned reader response, hence Tennyson conforms to the parameters of Victorian reader expectations. As Jauss puts it:

> the reconstruction of the horizon of expectations, on the basis of which a work in the past was created and received enables us to find the questions which the text originally answered and thereby to discover how the reader of that day viewed and understood the work. This approach corrects the usually unrecognized values of a classical conception of art or of an interpretation that seeks to modernize, and it avoids the recourse to a general spirit of the age, which involves circular reasoning. It brings out the hermeneutic difference between past and present ways of understanding a work . . . and thereby challenges as platonizing dogma the apparently self-evident dictum of philoloical metaphysics that literature is timelessly present and that it has objective meaning, determined once and for all and directly open to the interpreter at any time.[27]

Reader response theory, like new historicism, works on our recognizing the dialectical relationship between a text as product of a particular age and that text as received in another context. Jauss is explicitly opposed to what he calls the 'platonizing dogma' of the universal objective meaning of a text, and although some critics may have studied the recurrence of themes across cultures as an example of precisely this impossible ideal, thematic study today has no such pretensions. What we can see from the different versions of the Guinevere story is not simply that different writers work in different ways, but rather that those writers as products of their own time were mindful of the constraints laid upon them by the expectations of their readers. So Morris and Tennyson, fascinated as they are by the figure of the queen who chose to love another man, are nevertheless caught up in the problematic question of women's independence that was such a key issue in nineteenth-century England. The bitter struggle for women's right to own property in marriage went on for years, from the Married Women's Property Reform Bill which got as far as the House of Commons in 1855, to the eventual passing of a vastly truncated version of that bill in 1870. The struggle for voting rights and for the right of women to education lasted for decades and as we know from some of Tennyson's other writings, his contempt for women's education was by no means a secret.[28] Likewise Morris, utopian socialist though he was, had great personal difficulty in coping with his wife's love for Rossetti, as his writings also demonstrate. These tensions, which are partly due to individual circumstances and partly to the constraints of the wider social group, emerge in Morris' and Tennyson's depiction of Guinevere.

The convention of the romantic novel which underlies Gillian Bradshaw's treatment of the story requires women to find happiness and fulfilment within a relationship with a man. Her Guinevere, though the narrator of the book, is a passive, helpless character, remarkably unaware of her own powers and still unaware by the end, when she remarks almost in surprise that she has 'begun speaking like an abbess'. Weighed down by guilt, Bradshaw's Guinevere is an example of an archetypal romantic heroine, on whom fate acts, for she is not in control at any stage of her life or destiny. That such a novel could have been produced and been successful despite two decades of feminist thought and writing is evidence of the continued power of traditional images of subordinate femininity within the conventions of a particular literary type.

Of the texts considered here, it is Mallory's version that offers the most positive image of Guinevere. Feminist historians are still in the process of reassessing the evidence we have of the status of women in the pre-Renaissance world, for contrary to popular belief that status as evidenced by the right to own property, belong to guilds or have access to education would seem to have been higher than it was in the post-Renaissance world. Positivist thought, which so dominated the development of comparative literature in the nineteenth century, sought to show that the history of humanity had been a steady move forward from primitivism to enlightenment. By this reading, which stressed the significance of the Renaissance as a re-awakening from darkness, Mallory was accorded the status of a talented if crude story-teller, the product of a barbaric period though on the right track.

The notion of cultural history as the story of progress towards modernity derives in part from a belief in the superiority of the present. From that position, critics have looked back and constructed a canon of great works that stand like beacons along the road to enlightenment. The canon of English literature, for example, has Chaucer as a shining light and then a few small lamps such as Wyatt and Surrey until we reach the latter part of the sixteenth century and find Marlowe, Shakespeare and their contemporaries. This view of English literary history, which still conditions syllabus development, sees Mallory in an uncomfortable position in a time when not much writing of canonical status was seen to be happening. What it ignores completely, however, is the importance of other forms of writing, most especially translation. The fifteenth century was a period of intensive translation activity, and indeed a characteristic of the Renaissance is the large amount of translation taking place, from ancient and modern languages.

The retelling of the Arthurian material is also a process of translation, but just as translation studies is moving away from overly emphasizing the source text (or 'original' text) towards a consideration of the processes of production and designated readership of the target text, so the study of rewriting can offer new insights into literary history through a comparison of how, when and why those rewritings have taken place. The story of Guinevere viewed in this way opens up windows into differing moments in cultural history, exposing not only the overt details of what readers chose to read, but also the underlying assumptions encoded in each text about the status of women and their role within marriage.

7

From Comparative Literature to Translation Studies

The opening chapters of this book suggest that the term 'comparative literature' has declined in significance in recent years, although it has also been argued that comparative practice is alive and well and thriving under other nomenclature. In contrast, however, Translation Studies has been gaining ground, and since the end of the 1970s has come to be seen as a discipline in its own right, with professional associations, journals, publishers' catalogues and a proliferation of doctoral theses.

The relationship between comparative literature and the study of translation has been a complex and problematic one. Translation has tended to be regarded as the poor relation, as an activity involving little talent and creativity, as something that could be carried out by trained hacks and financially rewarded accordingly. Hilaire Belloc's view in his 1931 Taylorian Lecture sums up a situation that is still unhappily all too recognizable in some countries:

> The art of translation is a subsidiary art and derivative. On this account it has never been granted the dignity of original work, and has suffered too much in the general judgement of letters. This natural underestimation of its value has had the bad practical effect of lowering the standard demanded, and in some periods has almost destroyed the art altogether. The corresponding misunderstanding of its character has added to its degradation: neither its importance nor its difficulty has been grasped.[1]

Belloc's lecture was polemical, in that he wanted to remind his listeners of the complexity of the translation process with a view to raising its debased status. To that end he exaggerated the issues, for it is simply not true that translation had never 'been granted the dignity of original work'. The situation Belloc was referring to had developed gradually, from the seventeenth century onwards. Certainly by the nineteenth century, the status of a translation was generally considered to be lower than that of an 'original', and theorists of comparative literature, while acknowledging the role played by translation in their work, tended to assert the primacy of reading in original languages. Studies of comparative literature came increasingly to relegate translation to a single chapter or subsection, often placed together with terms such as 'adaptation' or 'imitation', all implicitly suggesting texts of a more derivative and secondary nature.

Binary comparative studies stood firmly against the idea of translation. A good comparatist, according to the binary model, would read original texts in the original languages, an infinitely superior form of reading than any which involved translation. The North American model, based on notions of universal values in literary texts, simply ignored the question of translation altogether; the processes whereby a text could be transferred from one context into another were either not regarded as a useful object of study, or seen as territory to be explored by linguists rather than literary scholars. The low status of translation was enshrined in other ways: in editorial practice of relegating 'translations' to a separate category, often marginalized with categories such as 'juvenilia' in editions of an author's works; in the poor remuneration for translation; in the ranking of translations as less than critical works when determining criteria for promotion.

In the 1970s a group of scholars began to emerge offering a different perspective on the study of translation. Led initially by Itamar Evan-Zohar from Tel Aviv, the group proposed to define their objective as 'Translation Studies'. In a paper entitled 'Translation Theory Today', Evan-Zohar began by summarizing prevailing views on translation, before going on to propose a systematic approach that would cut through the wooliness of a great deal of thinking about the translation process:

How many times have we been tortured by the clichés of the un-initiated, veteran or novice, that translation is never equal to the original, that languages differ from one another, that culture is 'also' involved with translation procedures, that when a translation is 'exact' it tends to be 'literal' and hence loses the 'spirit' of the original, that the 'meaning' of a text means both 'content' and 'style', and so on. Not to speak of such approaches where norms are either overtly or covertly stated, i.e. where we are told how translations should look or how they should be conceived of in terms of one or another evaluative norm.[2]

The words emphasized by Evan-Zohar are, of course, part of a discourse that prioritizes the original and sees the translation as an inferior copy, as something that loses a vital ingredient present only in that original. He draws attention to the inadequacy of such terminology, and mocks those critics he calls 'uninitiated, veteran or novice' who continue to think in those terms. What this paper exposes, as does the rest of his work on translation, is the prevalence of a curiously schizophrenic position of the literary world with regard to translation. In an age when Borges has suggested that the concept of the definitive text belongs only to religion or fatigue, and post-structuralist critics have shown the fallacy of believing in a single, definitive reading, discourse on translation went on talking about 'originals' and 'accuracy' and continued to make use of a terminology of negativity. Translation, it is suggested, 'betrays', 'traduces', 'diminishes', 'reduces', 'loses' parts of the original, translation is 'derivative', 'mechanical', 'secondary', poetry is lost in translation, certain writers are 'untranslatable'.

The notion of the translation as a betrayal of the original is particularly prevalent. Lori Chamberlain, one of a growing number of feminist translation scholars, draws attention to the sexualization of this terminology, pointing out that it appears

> perhaps most familiarly in the tag 'les belles infidèles' like women, the adage goes, translations should be either beautiful or faithful. The tag is made possible both by the rhyme in French and by the fact that the word 'traduction' is a feminine one, thus making 'les beaux infidèles' impossible. This tag owes its longevity – it was coined in the seventeenth century – to more than phonetic similarity; what gives it the appearance of truth is that it has captured a cultural complicity between the issues of fidelity in translation and in marriage. For 'les belles infidèles', fidelity is defined as an implicit contract between translation (as woman) and original (as husband, father, or author). However, the infamous 'double standard' operates here as it might have in traditional marriages: the 'unfaithful'

wife/translation is publicly tried for crimes the husband/original is by law incapable of committing. This contract, in short, makes it impossible for the original to be guilty of infidelity. Such an attitude betrays real anxiety about the problem of paternity and translation; it mimics the patrilineal kinship system where paternity – not maternity – legitimizes an offspring.[3]

Lori Chamberlain is making an important point here, stressing the cultural complicity between fidelity in translation and in marriage: it is no accident that a substantial number of feminist translation scholars such as myself, Barbara Johnson, Barbara Godard, Sherry Simon, Annie Brisset or Suzanne de Lotbinière-Harwood all began using metaphors of 'infidelity' or alternative marriage contract in their writings on translation in the 1980s, for all have been concerned with rethinking the view of translation that sets the original in a higher position that the text created for a new target audience.

The challenge to the original like the challenge to the canon or to the notion of correct, single reading is clearly part of a wide-ranging post-modernist strategy. Instead of reading for 'truth', we now read as decoders. Barbara Johnson has suggested that the whole activity of reading and rereading reveals ever more gaps and uncertainties:

> By rereading the texts of writers and philosophers that have made a difference to Western history, it might be possible to become aware of the repressions, the elisions, the contradictions and the linguistic slippages that have functioned unnoticed and that undercut the certainties those texts have been read as upholding.[4]

The way in which translation studies began to mount an offensive against the dominance of the original and the consequent relegation of translation to a position of subservience was initially through the work of Evan-Zohar and his colleagues, most notably Gideon Toury, on polysystems theory. For Evan-Zohar went much further than simply attacking the vagueness of the language surrounding translation. He noted that although translation appeared to have played a major role in the development of national cultures, this fact was almost ignored by historians of culture, and there was practically no research at all on the function of translated literature within a literary system. The Renaissance, for example, has generally been perceived as a time of intensive translation activity, yet any systematic assessment of what was translated, why, by whom and how had not taken place.

The radical implications of Evan-Zohar's polysystemic approach to translation were immediately clear. All kinds of questions could now be asked that had previously not seemed to be of significance: why do some cultures translate more and some less? What kind of texts get translated? What is the status of those texts in the target system and how does it compare to the status of the texts in the source system? What do we know about translation conventions and norms at given moments, and how do we assess translation as an innovatory force? What is the relationship in literary history between extensive translation activity and the production of texts claimed as canonical? What image do translators have of their work and how has that image been expressed figuratively? These and countless other questions testify to the great shift in perception which has taken place, in which far from being a secondary, marginal activity, translation could be considered as a primary shaping force within literary history.

In a paper written in 1976, Evan-Zohar argues that certain conditions determine high translation activity in a culture. He identifies three major cases: when a literature is in an early stage of development; when a literature perceives itself to be peripheral or 'weak' or both; when there are turning points or crises or literary vacuums.[5] Subsequent work has taken up these ideas, and developed them further through specific case studies. So, for example, Maria Tymoczko argues that translation played a central role in the great twelfth-century shift from epic to romance:

> The twelfth century marks one of the most significant transitions in Western culture: the shift from epic to romance. The change is one of poetics, of course; it represents the transition from traditional oral hero tale to written, author-innovated literature. The shift involves changes in larger literary elements such as genre and character typologies, as well as formal changes such as the development of new metres, rhetorical devices and the like. The transition is also an ideological one. It involves the turning from a warrior ethos to courtly codes and the celebration of romantic love.[6]

Tymoczko suggests that translation played a fundamental part in this shift, and points out that elements of romance can be traced in antecedent translations, and that romance emerged from a multicultural context. By focusing not only on poetics but also on the means of production, that is, by tracing the gradual move towards authored works written for named patrons, Tymoczko shows the significant role played by translation. The case of the move from epic to romance during the period that established the vulgar languages across Europe as literary languages accords with Evan-Zohar's hypothesis that translation activity is high when literatures are in an early stage of development.

Contemporary figures on translated texts as compiled from publishers lists offer a good example of the hypothesis that 'peripheral' literary systems translate a great deal, in contrast to those literary systems which perceive themselves as 'major'. The percentage of published translations into English, for example, contrasts sharply with the percentage of published translations into Swedish or Polish or Italian. Obviously this has to do with patterns of convention, which rapidly become established, and has also to do with the technological self-sufficiency of the English speaking world as a whole and with the rise since the Second World War of English as a world language. However, the figures quoted by Lawrence Venuti in 1992 show some startling disparities. His figures for Italy in the 1980s show 26 per cent of books published annually as translations, mainly from English, with a rise to 50 per cent, 70 per cent or even 90 per cent of an individual publisher's output when literary translation is considered. In sharp contrast, in the period between 1984 and 1990, translations accounted for only 3.5 per cent of books published annually in the United States, with an even lower figure of 2.5 per cent for Britain.[7] The steady decline in translation activity during the nineteenth century as Britain became an imperial power can be linked to changes in self-esteem and to a belief in the inherent superiority of the English literary system, as has been discussed earlier in this book.

The Czech revival in the early nineteenth century offers an example of an emergent national literature that seeks to extend its range of models through the means of translation. The Czech scholar Vladimír Macura has studied the role played by translation in the Czech revival, and points to the significance of translation as explicit cultural policy:

Translation was not seen as passive submission to cultural impulses from abroad; on the contrary, it was viewed as an active, even aggressive act, an appropriation of foreign cultural values . . . translation was seen as an invasion of rival territory, an invasion undertaken with the intent of capturing rich spoils of war. In his preface to his translations from Schiller, Jan Evangelista Purkeyně, the Czech writer who was to become a physiologist of world renown, tried to interpret translation as an immediate reaction against the destructive impact of foreign cultures, a literal act of revenge for the damages the Slavic world had suffered in the past: 'If (to the detriment of the Slavs) the Germans, Italians, and Hungarians try to denationalize both our common people and our higher classes, let us use a more noble way of retaliation, taking possession of anything excellent they have created in the world of the mind.'[8]

Macura goes on to suggest that this expropriative function was of such importance in the Czech revival that it conditioned the choice of texts selected for translation. He reinterprets the case of Jung-mann's translation of *Paradise Lost*, hotly debated by critics for decades, and argues that this translation was a conscious attempt to bring into a newly emergent literary system a text that represented an amalgam of different cultures (Christian, Jewish, pagan) united in an epic of human culture, and therefore that Milton's work had a symbolic function also as a means of stressing the universality of pan-Slavic origins.

This kind of scholarship, which often involves radical revisions of cultural and literary history, has been made possible by advances in translation studies, and by polysystems theory in particular. In a valuable essay published in 1985, the Belgian scholars José Lambert and Rik van Gorp endeavoured to summarize the possibilities offered by this approach. They list a number of areas of research that can be developed, which involve both detailed analysis of texts and of the means of production of those texts. Valuable areas of research, they suggest, include studying the vocabulary, style, poetical and rhetorical conventions of both source and target systems; analyzing how a translation is termed (i.e. whether it is presented as a translation, or as an 'adaptation', an 'imitation' or even an 'original') in the target system, and its role and status in that system; mapping the history of translation theory and criticism in particular literatures at particular times; studying the emergence of groups or schools of translators and the significance of such; tracing the role of translations in the development of a literary system, with a view to establishing whether translation plays a conservative or an innovative role, etc. Significantly, Lambert and Van Gorp note that 'The main advantage of the scheme is that it enables us to bypass a number of deep-rooted traditional ideas concerning translational 'fidelity' and even 'quality' which are mainly source-oriented and inevitably normative.'[9]

The essay by Lambert and van Gorp was published in 1985 in a collection of papers edited by Theo Hermans, entitled *The Manipulation of Literature*. The appearance of this collection marked another stage in the development of translation studies, for the focus of the book was on the idea of translation not only as a shaping force in literature but also as a primary manipulative textual strategy. Polysystems theory in its first stage was necessarily target system focused, principally to rebut the older notion of the primacy of the original and the secondary status of translation activity, but by the mid–1980s the first, more evangelical phase of research based on polysystems theory was becoming transformed into something else. Indeed, it is possible now to talk about three distinct stages in the development of translation studies. The first phase, heavily influenced by polysystems theory involved a series of direct challenges to the established discourse on translation. Decontextualized work in linguistics was challenged on the one hand, evaluative unsystematic work in literary studies was challenged on the other. Crucial to this stage were the often bitter debates on equivalance theory.

The traditional notion of translation, upon which the concept of the bilingual dictionary rests, is that translation between languages is possible because of the prior existence of a notional equivalence between systems. Despite the Sapir – Whorf hypothesis, which argued that

> No two languages are ever sufficiently similar to be considered as representing the same social reality. The worlds in which different societies live are distinct worlds, not merely the same world with different labels attached.[10]

generations of translators have wanted to believe in equivalence and have sought to define it in terms of sameness, sometimes arguing that that sameness could be interpreted in different ways and was open to negotiation, but nevertheless was possible. The obvious problem with a theory of equivalence as sameness is that it denies the existence of hierarchical relations between source and target texts and cultures and assumes that translation takes place on a vertical axis, between identically-placed systems. Polysystems theory, on the contrary, argues that systems are never identically positioned, and that notions of the superiority or inferiority of a text or of a literary system are always in play.

The second phase of translation studies moved beyond the challenge to previous discourses, and was principally concerned with mapping, with tracing patterns of translation activity at given moments in time. The emphasis in this phase was still predominantly on the target system, but a great deal of important historical research began to appear. A significant development in this second stage, which marks a definite move away from the overly structuralist origins of polysystems theory and a step on the road towards post-structuralist translation studies, has been the work carried out on the figurative language used by translators, as evidenced in their prefaces, correspondence and statements about their work generally.

The Manipulation of Literature volume also included a pioneering essay by Theo Hermans on Renaissance translators working in Dutch, English and French which categorizes their use of metaphors to describe their work and reveals clear patterns of thought.[11] Hermans shows how clusters of metaphors used by translators reflect their thinking about the role and status of translation in their own time. Predictable metaphors relating to rhetoric in general include following in footsteps, changing clothing, discovering treasure or alchemical transfer, and these metaphors also show a certain degree of ambiguity towards the source text, with the status of the text in its source system being significant in determining the attitude and strategies of the translator as well as the right of the target culture to possess it.

Mapping clusters of metaphors in use at a given point in time exposes dominant attitudes to the activity of translation. In the age that was characterized by the growth of the slave trade and by a shift in perceptions of European states towards the rest of the world, translation metaphors of the seventeenth century are very revealing. Perrot d'Ablancourt's preface to his translation of the *Annals of Tacitus*, for example, contains a statement that he has followed Tacitus 'step by step' and rather as a slave than as a companion,[12] while Dryden's dedication to his *Aeneid* states that 'slaves we are, and labour on another man's plantation; we dress the vineyard, but the wine is the owner's.'[13]

The translator as slave, the servant of the source text, is a powerful metaphor that endures well into the nineteenth century. Implicit in this metaphor is the idea of dominance of the source text author over the subservient target text. A relatively lone voice offering a different image of the translation process was a female translator, Madame de Gournay, who suggested in 1623 that to translate was

> to engender a work anew. Engender, I say, because (the ancient writers] have to be decomposed by profound and penetrating reflection, in order to be reconstituted by a similar process; just as meat must be decomposed in our stomachs in order to form our bodies.[14]

Fidelity to an original/husband as a metaphor for translation and the loyalty of the slave to the master both reflect profound changes in reading and writing in the post-Renaissance world. The voyages of discovery were altering perspectives, and the new world waiting to be penetrated and fertilized by the powerful European colonizing originals was consistently described, as has been discussed in earlier chapters, in sexual terms. Foucault points likewise to immense changes in language: 'In the sixteenth century, one asked oneself how it was possible to know that a sign did in fact designate what it signified; from the seventeenth century, one began to ask how a sign could be linked to what it signified.'[15]

Current work on the metaphoric language of translators is an important aspect of the third phase of translation studies. A good deal of work in the early 1980s, though claiming to be non-normative, was still quite attached to statements, diagrams, charts and assertions about translation practice, which testified to the structuralist origins of the polysystems group. However, by the advent of the 'manipulation school' in the mid-eighties, work in the field of translation studies as a whole had diversified enormously. This third phase, which could be termed the post-structuralist stage, conceives of translation as one of a range of processes of textual manipulation, where the concept of plurality replaces dogmas of faithfulness to a source text, and where the idea of the original is being challenged from a variety of perspectives.

André Lefevere, for example, proposes that translation should be studied alongside what he calls 'rewritings', since

> rewriting, be it in the form of criticism or of translation (and, I might add, of historiography and anthologization), turns out to be

a very important strategy which guardians of a literature use to adapt what is 'foreign' (in time and/or geographical location) to the norms of the receiving culture. As such, rewriting plays a highly important part in the development of literary systems. On another level, rewritings are evidence of reception, and can be analysed as such. These would appear to be two perfectly good reasons to give the study of rewriting a more central status in both literary theory and comparative literature.[16]

Lefevere's argument is a persuasive one; translation needs to be seen as an important literary strategy, and the examination of translations within a framework of rewriting will reveal patterns of change in reception in a given literary system. He also draws attention to the importance of the role of historiography and anthologization, another growth area of research in translation studies, as the work of Armin Paul Frank and his colleagues at Göttingen testifies.[17]

The advent of polysystems theory in the early 1970s introduced ideology into the study of translation. Lefevere's early attempt at a manifesto for the emergent discipline of translation studies in 1976 stresses that important distinction:

> The goal of the discipline is to produce a comprehensive theory which can also be used as a guideline for the production of translations. The theory would gain by being developed along lines of argument which are neither neopositivist nor hermeneutic in inspiraton . . . and constantly tested by case-histories.[18]

Fifteen years later, Bassnett and Lefevere restate that goal, now in the light of the huge developments in the intervening period:

> with the development of Translation Studies as a discipline in its own right, with a methodology that draws on comparatistics and cultural history. Translation has been a major shaping force in the development of world culture and no study of comparative literature can take place without regard to translation.[19]

The advances in history of translation, in terms of the history of translation techniques, the production, distribution and financing of translations, schools or groups of translators and the role played by translations at given moments have finally shed light on the problem of terminology. The emphasis on 'accuracy' and on 'faithfulness' would appear to derive from seventeenth-century attitudes to the activity of translating. 'Accuracy' connotes the scientific, the precise, that which can be measured and quantified, while 'faithfulness' has dual implications: the good wife is faithful to her husband, and the good servant faithful to his master, both being in a position of inferiority vis-à-vis the original text.

It is in the seventeenth century that we suddenly find different types of interlingual transfer activity all being described in the same way. Translation, as referred to by those writers engaged in translating classical texts, is an activity involving great literary sensitivity. Dryden, for example, although referring to the translator as the slave of the original in the passage cited above, also states in his preface to the *Life of Lucian* in 1711 that a translator

> ought to possess himself entirely and perfectly comprehend the genius and sense of his author, the nature of the subject, and the terms of the art of subject treated of. And then he will express himself as justly, and with as much life, as if he wrote an original; whereas he who copies word for word loses all the spirit in the tedious transfusion.[20]

The key word here is 'possession'. The translator, Dryden argues, must possess himself of everything the author has to offer, for only then will he create something with as much life as an original. The implication here is that a translation can indeed become an original in its own right, though not if the translator 'copies' word for word.

What might at first appear to be a conflict of views expressed by the same writer is, in fact, simply recognition of different types of translation activity. The development of bilingual dictionaries, of grammar books and text books for languagelearning based on word for word transfer between languages resulted in the application of a form of translation within education systems based on quantifiable accuracy. In order to measure the student's competence in learning another language, the 'accuracy' of the translation as a word for word rendering of the source text is required. Yet at the same time, as Dryden recognizes, that same technique applied to the translation of poetry would be disastrous.

The need for 'accuracy' in translation used as an instrument in the teaching of a foreign language was established early and has remained with us. The problem we are left with however, is that the activity of translating a text in order to demonstrate competence in the source or target language in terms of understanding grammar and syntax is not the same thing as translating in the sense of decoding and reencoding a literary text, even though the terminology is the same for both. Moreover, in the seventeenth century the changes in mass production of books and the emergence of a new market of readers meant that the production of literary texts rapidly became big business. A similar process was taking place in theatres, and it is notable that a large number of plays performed on the London stages from the late seventeenth century onwards were translations. To meet the demands of the market place, those translations were often made at speed and by people with minimal competence. The disparity between the kind of translation work that involved classical texts and the mass-market translating of saleable texts was commented upon endlessly by contemporary critics, though once again the terminology describing these activities remained the same.

The confusion caused by use of the same terminology to describe translation as a high status literary activity, translation as a pedagogic instrument and translation as hack work for the mass market is still with us today, and helps to explain some of the conflicting feelings about the whole activity of translation. What we have is a legacy of confused histories, so that the very term 'translation' triggers differing sets of responses, related to different sets of assumptions and expectations about the activity of translating. Interestingly, it is the pedagogic role that seems to have acquired the greatest power, for it is here that the idea of accuracy as something that can be measured is all-important.

Ezra Pound comments on the fallacy of applying such criteria to literary translation:

> I ruined my English prose for five years, trying to write English as Tacitus wrote Latin. *Very bad*. However, I may have learned something by it. I now know that the genius of the two languages is not the same.[21]

Elsewhere, responding to attacks by scholars on the 'inaccuracy' of his *Homage to Sextus Propertius* as a translation, he defended his work:

> there never was any question of translation, let alone literal translation. My job was to bring a dead man to life, to present a living

figure. As a Prof. of Latin and example of why Latin poets are not read, as example of why one would like to deliver poets of philologers, Hale [Pound's most vitriolic opponent] should be impeccable and without error. He has NO claim to refrain from suicide if he errs in any point . . . mask of erudition is precisely what I have not assumed; it is precisely what I have thrown on the dust heap.[22]

Pound defends his work through a very deliberate metaphor: that of bringing a dead man back to life. His concept of translation is target focused, he sees his task as that of finding a readership for a dead poet. In this, Pound's view of the task of the translator connects with that of Walter Benjamin, who, in his famous introduction to the German translation of Baudelaire's *Tableux Parisiens* (1923) also uses the metaphor of the translation as afterlife. Benjamin's essay was rediscovered by translation theorists in the 1980s, and has become one of the most significant texts of post-modern translation theory. Derrida's reading of Benjamin, in his essay 'Des Tours de Babel' (1985) plays with ideas of original and translation, with the problem of where meaning is located. What he suggests is a further radical attack on the idea of the primacy of the original. The source text, according to Derrida, is not an original at all, it is the elaboration of an idea, of a meaning, in short it is in itself a translation. The logical consequences of Derrida's thinking about translation would be the abolition of the dichotomy between original and translation, between source and copy, and hence an end to the view that relegates translation to a secondary position.[23] Benjamin had already proclaimed the life-enhancing role of translation as a transformative process: 'a translation comes later than the original, and since the important works of world literature never find their chosen translators at the time of their origin, their translation marks their stage of continued life.'[24] Translation is therefore a particularly special activity, since it enables a text to continue life in another context, and the translated text becomes an original by virtue of its continued existence in that new context.

The interest shown by Derrida and other contemporary philosophers is a further sign of the growing significance of translation,[25] and of the increasing interdisciplinarity of work in translation studies. And with the growing number of studies on aspects of translation by philosophers, literary and cultural historians, sociolinguists and literary theorists, so the negative terminology that has dominated discussion of translation is finally beginning to disappear. There is a world of difference between old-style complaints about the loss factor in translation and the new notion of translation as conferring new life on the source text. Moreover, as translation historians discover more about the genealogy of translation, so increasingly does the inter-lingual transfer of texts appear as a vital component in cultural development.

The scholars following Evan-Zohar and the polysystems school have tended to be European based, with some also in the United States, and have tended to concern themselves primarily with history. It is interesting to compare the rise and rise of translation history with a similar process that is ongoing in women's studies, and in both these cases the result is constant revision of many of our assumptions about literary and cultural history. In chapter 6 it was suggested that there might be an alternative way of looking at, for example, the fifteenth century, traditionally considered a fallow period in English literature because it produced no 'great' writers. By shifting perspective slightly, and noting the high production of translations in this period, we now look at the fifteenth century as a classic example of an age in the process of looking outwards for literary models and using translators as a means of revitalizing the target system. There is not a substantial body of work on medieval and Renaissance translation, looking not only at strategies employed by translators but also at the role played by translations in the development of literary systems.[26]

Earlier in this book, it was pointed out that a great deal of exciting, innovative comparative work is taking place outside Europe, often under different names than those traditionally used by European academics, and the same can also be said of work in translation studies. Of special significance are the theories of translation currently proposed by translators in Brazil and in Canada, which offer new metaphors and new perspectives on the significance of the translation process.

Post-colonial theory is concerned with analysing the aftermath; it is concerned with reconstruction and reassessment, which necessarily involves a translation process. Ashcroft *et al.* state that

> post-colonial culture is inevitably a hybridized phenomenon involving a dialectical relationship between the 'grafted' European cultural systems and an indigenous ontology, with its impulse to

create or recreate an independent local identity. Such construction or reconstruction only occurs as a dynamic interaction between European hegemonic systems and 'peripheral' subversions of them. It is not possible to return to or to rediscover an absolute pre-colonial cultural purity, nor is it possible to create national or regional formations entirely independent of their historical implications in the European colonial enterprise.[27]

What they are suggesting here is that there can be no such thing as an original, and that post-colonial culture involves a dialectical relationship between systems. In the case of Latin America, it is significant that accounts of the earliest process of colonization involve a translator seen both as betrayer and as helpmate. La Malinche, Cortés' mistress/interpreter, is a figure who symbolizes the Janus-face of translation: one version of her life presents her as a noble Indian woman who lived with Cortés and endeavoured to bring her own people together with her lover's compatriots. Another version sees her as betraying her own people to the invaders, providing the linguistic bridge necessary for them to devastate Mexican civilization. Yet another version sees her as the victim of rape, compelled to serve the colonial master, forced to act as unwilling intermediary in the larger process of violation of a society.

The ambiguity of interpretations of La Malinche's role in the early stages of colonization is mirrored in the long listing of ambiguity experienced by Latin American writers and critics towards Europe, the source of literary models, the Original. Recently, it has been suggested that Latin America can be seen as a 'translation' of Europe, though with translation understood in the sense argued by Benjamin and Derrida, that is, as an after-life, a survival, a continuation through renascence, and not as a copy.[28]

In the 1920s, Brazilian Modernism proposed a reevaluation of the ultimate European taboo: cannibalism. Oswald de Andrade's 'Manifesto Antropófago'[29] considered the case of the Portuguese bishop, eaten in a cannibalistic ritual by Brazilian Indians in 1554, and pointed out that there are two entirely different ways of understanding this event. From the European perspective, it was an abomination, an act of sacrilege, a violation of every norm of civilized behaviour. However appalling the torture chambers of the Inquisition back in Europe may have been, the torturers stopped short of eating their victims. But considered from the non-European perspective, the act of eating a person one respects in order to absorb their strength or virtues through the sacrifice was perfectly acceptable. Moreover, the basic premise of the Mass involves the symbolic swallowing of the Body and Blood of Christ, so to a culture that accepts cannibalism as an act of respect, Christianity could be interpreted very differently. The Antropófagista Movement saw in this dual perspective a metaphor for the relationship between European and Brazilian cultures. As Randall Johnson puts it:

> Metaphorically speaking, it represents a new attitude towards cultural relationships with hegemonic powers. Imitation and influence in the traditional sense of the word are no longer possible. *The antropófagos* do not want to copy European culture, but rather to devour it, taking advantage of its positive aspects, rejecting the negative, and creating an original, national culture that would be a source of artistic expression rather than a receptacle for forms of cultural expression elaborated elsewhere.[30]

It is easy to see how this metaphor came later to be adapted by translation scholars. The *antropófagos* suggested that the European models should be devoured, so that their virtues would then pass into the works of Brazilian writers. Through this image the power relationship between European culture and Brazilian is transformed; the Brazilian writer is not an imitator, not subservient in any way to the European literary tradition, nor does protest involve a rejection of that tradition altogether. Rather, the Brazilian writer interacts with the source culture, drawing upon it for nourishment but creating something entirely new. Where translaton is concerned, the metaphor acquires special resonance, for the translator devours the source text and engenders it anew, just as Madame de Gournay suggested nearly four centuries ago.

Haraldo and Augusto de Campos have been the principal practitioners and theoreticians of the cannibalistic concept of translation. Their work deliberately erases boundaries between sources and target systems, so that Haraldo de Campos' translation of Goethe's *Faust*, published in 1979, is entitled *Deus e o diabo no Fausto de Goethe* [God and the devil in Goethe's Faust]. This title emphasizes the link between Goethe the writer and his Faustus, while referring directly to the subject of the work, the clash between the diabolical and the divine. It also resolutely asserts the presence of the translator/writer and his relationship to the German creator of Faust. But for Brazilian readers it also signifies something else: it is a direct reference to Glauber Rocha's film, *Deus e o Diabo na Terra do Sol* [God and the devil in the country of the sun].[31] As Else Veira points out:

> The interest in the very title suggests that the 'receiving' culture will interpenetrate and transform the original one . . . from the title we can say that translation is no longer a one-way flow from the source to the target culture, but a two-way transcultural enterprise.[32]

Moreover, de Campos does not describe his undertaking as a 'translation' but as a 'transluciferaçao mefistofaustico' and he argues that this kind of diabolical undertaking 'intends to erase the origin, to obliterate the original'.[33] Translation is for him a physical process, it is a devouring of the source text, a transmutation process, an act of vampirization. Translation, as he says, 'come transfusao. De sangue' [translation as transfusion. Of blood].[34]

The images of translation as cannibalism, as vampirism, whereby the translator sucks out the blood of the source text to strengthen the target text, as transfusion of blood that endows the receiver with new life, can all be seen as radical metaphors that spring from post-modernist post-colonial translation theory. Significantly, they link up with other developments in translation theory discussed above, for what all have in common is a rejection of the power hierarchy which privileged the source text and relegated the translator to a secondary role. Else Veira sums up the significance of the can-nibalistic theory for translation practice:

> The cannibalistic translational philosophy of nourishing from two reservoirs, the source text and the target literature, and, to the same extent, the reverse reading of translation operated by Benjamin and Derrida exposes a number of epistemological questions that tradi-tional traductology is unfit to answer. Or, using Benjamin's terms, traditional traductology demands a translation, a revision . . . if, in the cannibalist philosophy, translation becomes a two-way flow, the very terminology 'source' and 'target' becomes depleted. By the same token, the power relation between source and target, superior/ inferior ceases to exist.[35]

The new work in Brazilian translation studies is characterized by a series of physical metaphors, often violent ones, that stand out in sharp contrast to the gentler metaphors describing translation as a servile activity. Similarly, developments in the field in Canada from the mid–1980s onwards have also stressed the physical, though primarily in terms of redefined sexual relations, perceived from a feminist perspective.

Hélène Cixous has suggested that 'feminine' writing takes place in between the two poles of male and female: 'Writing is precisely working (in) the in-between inspecting the process of the same and the other without which nothing can live, undoing the work of death.'[36] Feminist translation theorists have built upon Cixous's notion of in-betweenness, developing it in new ways. Nicole Ward-Jouve, for example, a bilingual, bicultural writer and critic, comments that:

> The translator is a being in-between. Like words in translation, s/he endlessly drifts between meanings. S/he tries to be the go-between, to cunningly suggest what readings there could be in the foreign language other than those the chosen translation makes available . . . You are led to reflect on how particular translations become constructed. What gets lost, what is gained, what and how altered, in the passage from one language to the next.[37]

The old binary notion of translation saw original and translated texts as two poles. Feminist translation theory focuses d on the interactive space between the two poles, and notes that those poles have long been interpreted in terms of masculine and feminine. The basis of the 'belles infidèles' metaphor is that the source, the original is masculine and all-powerful, while the target text is feminine and subservient. Feminist translation theory, by celebrating the in-betweenness, reconstructs the space in which the translation takes place as bi-sexual, belonging neither to one nor to the other.

Some of the most exciting feminist work on translation in Canada has centred around lesbian or bisexual theorists and translators. The group working with and around Nicole Brossard, for example, reject both writer-oriented criticism and the newer reader-oriented criticism, arguing that neither writer nor reader should be prioritized. Kathy Mezei describes the translation process as 'a compound act of reading and writing', recognizing that the translator is both reader and writer: 'When I translate I read the text . . . then I reread the text and I reread the text, and then I write in my language, my words: I write my reading and the reading has rewritten my writing.'[38] This is a very different idea of translation from that proposed by George Steiner, who sees translation as involving the 'appropriative penetration' of the source text, so that the text is 'captured' and the translator then compensates for the act of aggression by a gesture of restitution.[39]

Another Canadian translation scholar, Barbara Godard, has made the connection between feminist translation work and postmodernist translation theory, arguing that although it has traditionally been a negative topos in translation, 'difference' is positive in feminist translation:

> As feminist theory has been concerned to show, difference is a key factor in cognitive processes and in critical praxis . . . The feminist translator affirming her critical difference, her delight in interminable rereading and rewriting, flaunts the signs of her manipulation of the text. Womanhandling the text in translation would involve the replacement of the modest, self-effacing translator.[40]

The feminist translator, Godard proclaims, is immodest, flaunting her possession and repossession of the text. Her translator is not self-effacing, and like the Brazilian 'luciferizing' translators, she asserts her right to shape and manipulate the source text. Suzanne de Lotbinière-Harwood, another of the Canadian translation school, proclaims that her translation practice is a political activity, and that 'translation is an act of linguistic invention which often enriches the original text instead of betraying it'.[41]

The Brazilian and the Canadian groups of translation theorists have in common the aim of celebrating the role of the translator, of making the translator visible in an act of transgression that seeks to reconstruct the old patriarchal/European hierarchies. Translation seen in their terms is indeed a political activity, and one of the utmost importance. Haraldo and Augusto de Campos use translation as a way of affirming their right as Brazilians to reread and repossess canonical European literature, while the Canadian women see translation as fundamental to their existence as bilinguals and as feminists struggling against phallo/logocentric values. Both groups are concerned to find a translation practice and terminology that will convey the rupture with the dominance of the European heritage even as it is transmitted. In their different ways, one group with the metaphoric language of blood and death, the other with a series of metaphors deriving from the notion of the 'mother-tongue', are proposing a post-colonial notion of translation, which contests the old imperialist view. As Henri Meschonnic reminds us: 'Cultural imperialism tends to forget its own history, to the point of failing to recognize the role of translation on culture.'[42] Radical reconsideration of translation is therefore a fundamental element of post-imperialist literary studies. Cultural history considered through the history of translations and their reception in the target context can shed new light on the inter-relationship between literature, besides challenging canonical hierarchies of 'major' and 'minor' authors, or greater and lesser periods of literary activity. Polysystems theory as proposed by Evan-Zohar has offered one way towards that reconsideration process, but equally, the work of the bilingual Canadian feminist translators and that of the Brazilian school show that there are alternative methods of challenging the traditional marginalization of translation. Evan-Zohar offered a new way of thinking about literary history; the de Campos brothers offer a new way of thinking about the relationship between source and target texts by prioritizing the role of the translator in that relationship, while Nicole Brossard and Suzanne de Lotbinière-Harwood reject any idea of binary oppositions and explore the dynamic space that lies in between.

The extraordinary range of work at present taking place in the field of translation studies, the new journals coming into being, the proliferation of international conferences, the number of books being written and doctoral theses being produced testify to the vitality of this previously marginal and unrespected field of study. Because it draws on different methodologies, translation studies has become a genuinely interdisciplinary field, and it may be that a better way to describe it would be to use a term like Intercultural Studies. It is also difficult now to see it merely as a sub-category of comparative literature, partly because the term 'comparative literature', as this book has sought to show, has little meaning today (not that it ever had much meaning from the outset), and partly because it is such a dynamic subject area, while comparative leterature as a formalist exercise is in decline.

There are, of course, different schools of thought about the relationship between translation studies and comparative literature. There are those who still see translation as a marginal activity, rejecting the propositions of the polysystems group and holding to a notion of literature as a universal civilizing force. Such scholars tend obviously to be Eurocentric in outlook, and continue to believe in the continuity of a canon of 'great' works. Then there are also those who argue that translation studies should shake off its links with comparative literature altogether, that the two have nothing in common and have different concerns and methodologies. Comparative literature, they would argue, is still caught up in formalist coils, still struggling with its state of constant crisis, and enmeshment with this state of uneasiness can only damage the newly emergent discipline of translation studies, the proper concerns of which are historical and linguistic.

Neither of these positions seems worth pursuing. This book has sought to show that the crisis of comparative literature derives from a legacy of nineteenth-century Eurocentric positivism and from a refusal to consider the political implications of intercultural transfer, which are fundamental to any comparative activity. It has also been argued that the so-called crisis is not being experienced by African, Indian, Chinese, or Latin American comparatists because they have constructed comparative literary studies from a different ideological base, taking as a starting point not an abstract idea of transcultural universal beauty but the immediate needs of their own culture. And one crucial, consistently experienced need is the enrichment and development of the national language (or languages). Polysystems theory offers a way of looking at that process of development not in terms of influences or movements, but in concrete terms of translation policy and translational strategies. What is translated, when and by whom, how it is received and what its status then becomes in the target culture are fundamental questions, but have begun to be asked not by those calling themselves comparative literature specialists, but by those claiming to work in translation studies. For translation has to do with authority and with power, and as André Lefevere puts it:

> Translation is not just 'a window opened on another world', or some such pious platitude. Rather, translation is a channel opened, often not without a certain reluctance, through which foreign influences can penetrate the native culture, challenge it and even contribute to subverting it.[43]

In their introduction to the collection of essays entitled *Translation, History and Culture* (1990) Bassnett and Lefevere argue that the time has come to rethink the marginalization of translation within comparative literature:

> with the development of Translation Studies as a discipline in its own right, with a methodology that draws on comparatistics and cultural history, the time has come to think again. Translation has been a major shaping force in the develoment of world culture, and no study of comparative literature can take place without regard to translation.[44]

As comparative literature continues to argue about whether it can be considered a discipline or not, translation studies states boldly that it *is* a discipline, and the strength and energy of work in the field world-wide seem to confirm that assertion. The time has come for a reconsideration of the relationship between comparative literature and translation studies, and for a new beginning.

In 1979, Heidi Hartmann's essay entitled 'The Unhappy Marriage of Marxism and Feminism' wittily set out a series of problems using the metaphor of marriage.[45] Can the relationship be healed, she asked, or has the time come for a divorce? We might well borrow that metaphor for the relationship between comparative literature and translation studes, where there has traditionally been a dominant and subservient partner, with Literature superior to translation. A redefinition of the relationship would alter that balance of power, and would see translation studies as the principle partner, with comparative literature no longer dominant. This would make sense not only in terms of the different state of current research in these two fields, but also in terms of the different objects of study. For comparative literature has struggled and struggled to define itself, insisting variously on upholding certain values and rejecting calls for clearer definitions of scope and methodology, while translation studies has concerned itself with texts and with contexts, with practice and with theory, with diachronics and synchronics and above all with the manipulative process of intercultural transfer and its ideological implications.

As we come to the end of the twentieth century, it is surely time to recognize that an era is over. Writing does not happen in a vacuum, it happens in a context and the process of translating texts from one cultural system into another is not a neutral, innocent, transparent activity. Translation is instead a highly charged, transgressive activity, and the politics of translation and translating deserve much greater attention than has been paid in the past. Translation has played a fundamental role in cultural change, and as we consider the diachronics of translation practice we can learn a great deal about the position of receiving cultures in relation to source text cultures.

Comparative literature as a discipline has had its day. Cross-cultural work in women's studies, in post- colonial theory, in cultural studies has changed the face of literary studies generally. We should look upon translation studies as the principal discipline from now on, with comparative literature as a valued but subsidiary subject area.

Notes

INTRODUCTION: WHAT IS COMPARATIVE LITERATURE TODAY?

1 Matthew Arnold, *On the Modern Element in Literature*, Inaugural Lecture delivered in the University of Oxford, 14 November 1857.

2 Johann W. von Goethe, 'Some Passages Pertaining to the Concept of World Literature', in Hans Joachim Schultz and Phillip H. Rhein (eds) *Comparative Literature: The Early Years*, Chapel Hill, University of North Carolina Press, 1973, pp. 3–11.

3 René Wellek, 'The Crisis of Comparative Literature', in *Concepts of Criticism*, New Haven and London, Yale University Press, 1963, pp. 282–96.

4 Benedetto Croce, 'Comparative Literature', in Schultz and Rhein, 1973, pp. 215–23.

5 Croce, p. 222.

6 Charles Mills Gayley, 'What is Comparative Literature?' *Atlantic Monthly*, 92 (1903), pp. 56–68.

7 François Jost, *Introduction to Comparative Literature*, Indianapolis, Bobbs-Merrill, 1974, pp. 29–30.

8 René Wellek and Austin Warren, *Theory of Literature*, London, Jonathan Cape, 1949, p. 44.

9 Harry Levin, *Comparing the Literature*, Presidential Address at the meeting of the American Comparative Literature Association, Indiana University, 1968. Publ. in *Grounds for Comparison*, Cambridge, Mass., Harvard University Press, 1972, pp. 74–90.

10 Swapan Majumdar, *Comparative Literature: Indian Dimensions*, Calcutta, Papyrus, 1987, p. 53.

11 Ganesh Devy, 'Comparative Literature in India', *New Quest*, no. 63, May–June 1987, pp. 133–147.

12 Homi Bhabha, 'Articulating the Archaic: Notes on Colonial Non-sense', in Peter Collier and Helga Geyer-Ryan (eds), *Literary Theory*

Today, Cambridge, Polity Press, 1990, pp. 203–19.

13 James Snead, 'Repetition as a figure of black culture', in Harry Louis Gates Jr. (ed.) *Black Literature and Literary Theory*, New York and London, Methuen, 1984, pp. 59–80.

14 Terry Eagleton, *Literary Theory: An Introduction*, Oxford, Blackwell, 1983, p. 22.

15 Eagleton, p. 30.

16 Edward Said, *Orientalism*, London, Routledge and Kegan Paul, 1978, p. 203.

17 Zhang Longxi, 'The Myth of the Other: China in the Eyes of the West,' in Yang Zhouhan and Yue Daiyun (eds) *Cultural Interflow East and West: Literatures, Histories and Literary Histories*, Shenyang, University of Liaoning Press, 1989, pp. 188–223.

18 Bill Ashcroft, Gareth Griffiths and Helen Tiffin, *The Empire Writes Back: Theory and Practice in Post-Colonial Literatures*, London and New York, Routledge, 1989, p. 2.

19 See: Itamar Evan-Zohar, 'Polysystems Theory', *Poetics Today* I, 2 (Autumn, 1979) pp. 237–310. Theo Hermans (ed.), *The Manipulation of Literature*, London, Croom Helm, 1985. Gideon Toury, *In Search of a Theory of Translation*, Tel Aviv, the Porter Institute for Poetics and Semiotics, 1980.

CHAPTER 1   HOW COMPARATIVE LITERATURE CAME INTO BEING

1 René Wellek, 'The Name and Nature of Comparative Literature', *Discriminations*, New Haven and London, Yale University Press, 1970, pp. 1–36.

2 Matthew Arnold, letter to his sister, May 1848, cited in Siegbert Prawer, *Comparative Literary Studies: An Introduction*, London, Duckworth, 1973.

3 Cours de M. Philarète Chasles à l'Athénée. Séance d'ouverture, 17 janvier, 1835. Pub. in *Revue de Paris*, XIII, no. 17, 1835, pp. 238–62. English version in H. J. Schulz and P. H. Rhein (eds), *Comparative Literature: The Early Years*, Chapel Hill, The University of North Carolina Press, 1973, pp. 13–39.

4 Byron, Preface to *The Prophecy of Dante*, 1819, *The Poetical Works of Lord Byron*, London, Oxford University Press, 1959, p. 37.

5 Vladimír Macura, 'Culture as Translation', in Susan Bassnett and Andre Lefevere (eds) *Translation, History and Culture*, London, Pinter, 1990, pp. 64–71.

6 See Timothy Brennan, 'The National Longing for Form', in Homi K. Bhabha (ed.) *Nation and Narration*, London, Routledge, 1990, pp. 44–71.

7 Frédéric Lolliée, *A Short History of Comparative Literature from the Earliest Times to the Present Day*, trans. M. Douglas Power, London, Hodder and Stoughton, 1906, p. 79.

8 Minute addressed by Lord Macaulay to Lord Bentinck, Governor General of India, 2 Feb. 1835. Reprinted in Philip D. Curtin (ed.) *Imperialism: The Documentary History of Western Civilization*, New York, Walker & Col., 1971, pp. 178–91.

9 Edward Fitzgerald, letter to Cowell, 20 March 1857.

10 Jawaharlal Nehru, 'The Economic Background of India: The Two Englands', *The Discovery of India*, New Delhi, 1981, p. 287.

11 C. L. Wrenn, *The Idea of Comparative Literature*, pamphlet publ. by the Modern Humanities Research Association, 1968, p. 5.

12 Chasles, 1835.

13 Ulrich Weisstein, *Comparative Literature and Literary Theory*, Bloomington, Indiana University Press, 1973, p. 171.

14 Paul Van Tieghem, *La Littérature Comparée*, Paris, Colin, 1931, p. 57 (cited in English in Weisstein, 1973, p. 5).

15 Ferdinand Brunetière, 'European Literature', *Revue des deux mondes* 161 (1900), pp. 326–55, in Joachim Schultz and Phillip Rhein (eds) *Comparative Literature: The Early Years*, Chapel Hill, University of North Carolina Press, 1973, pp. 153–82.

16 Max Koch, Introduction to *Zeitschrift für vergleichende Literaturgeschichte*, I.O.S. (1887), pp. 1–12, in Schultz and Rhein, pp. 63–77. 21 Van Tieghem, 1931. See Weisstein, 1973, p. 4.

17 Van Tieghem, 1931. See Weisstein, 1973, p. 4.

18 Weisstein, 1973, p. 200.

19 Hugo Meltzl de Lomnitz, 'Present Tasks of Comparative Literature', in Schultz and Rhein, pp. 53–62.

20 Lolliée, pp. 226–7.

21 René Wellek, p. 17.

22 Weisstein, 1973, pp. 13–14.

23 René Wellek, 'The Crisis of Comparative Literature', in *Concepts of Criticism*, New Haven, Yale University Press, 1963, pp. 282–96.

CHAPTER 2   BEYOND THE FRONTIERS OF EUROPE

1 Henry Remak, 'Comparative Literature, Its Definition and Function', in Newton Stallknecht and Horst Frenz (eds), *Comparative Literature: Method and Perspective*, Carbondale, Southern Illinois Press, 1961, p. 3.

2 Remak, p. 7.

3 Remak, p. 3.

4 Charles Mills Gayley, 'What is Comparative Literature?', in *The Atlantic Monthly*, 92, 1903, pp. 56–68. Reprinted in Joachim Schulz and Phillip Rhein (eds) *Comparative Literature: The Early Years*, Chapel Hill, University of North Carolina Press, 1973, p. 102.

5 Hutcheson Macaulay Posnett, 'The Science of Comparative Literature', *The Contemporary Review*, 79, 1901, pp. 855–72, reprinted in Schulz and Rhein, p. 188.

6 Posnett, p. 197.

7 Arthur Richmond Marsh, 'The Comparative Study of Literature', *PMLA*, 11, no. 2, 1896, pp. 151–70, reprinted in Schulz and Rhein, p. 128.

8 Fredric Jameson, *The Prison-House of Language*, Princeton, Princeton University Press, 1972, p. 45.

9 René Wellek, 'The Name and Nature of Comparative Literature', *Discriminations*, New Haven and London, Yale University Press, 1970, pp. 20–1.

10 Ulrich Weisstein, *Comparative Literature and Literary Theory*, Bloomington, Indiana University Press, 1968, pp. 13–14.

11 Weisstein, p. 13.

12 Swapan Majumdar, *Comparative Literature, Indian Dimensions*, Calcutta, Papyrus, 1987, p. 54.

13 Majumdar, p. 54.

14 Sri Aurobindo, *The Human Cycle*, Ashram, Pondicherry, 1943, p. 83.

15 Chidi Amuta, *The Theory of African Literature*, London, Zed Books, 1989, p. 19.

16 Chinua Achebe, *Morning Yet on Creation Day*, London, Heinemann, 1975, p. 9.

17 Kimberley W. Benston, 'I yam what I am: the topos of (un)naming in Afro-American literature', in Henry Louis Gates Jr. (ed.), *Black Literature and Literary Theory*, New York and London, Methuen, 1984, pp. 151–75.

18 Sigmund Freud, *Group Psychology and the Analysis of the Ego*, trans. James Strachey, New York, Norton, 1959, pp. 33–4.

19 Siegbert Prawer, *Comparative Literary Studies: An Introduction*, London, Duckworth, 1973, p. 102.

20 Henry Gifford, *Comparative Literature*, London, 1969, p. 73.

21 Richard Johnson, 'The story so far: and further transformations?', in David Punter (ed.), *Introduction to Contemporary Cultural Studies*, London, Longman, 1986, pp. 277–314.

CHAPTER 3 COMPARING THE LITERATURES OF THE BRITISH ISLES

1 Seamus Heaney, 'An Open Letter', in Field Day Theatre Company, *Ireland's Field Day*, London, Hutchinson, 1985, pp. 23–30.
2 Glanville Price, The Languages of Britain, London, Edward Arnold, 1984.
3 Price, p. 186.
4 Henry Wyld, *The Growth of English*, London, Murray, 1907, p. 48.
5 George Sampson, *English for the English*, London, 1925, p. 41.
6 Saunders Lewis, 'Byd a Betws' (1941), cited in Thomas Parry, A History of Welsh Literature, trans. H. Idris Bell, Oxford, Clarendon, 1955, p. 412.
7 Hugh Macdiarmid, from 'A Drunk Man Looks at the Thistle', in M. Grieve and W. Aitken (eds), *Complete Poems*, London, Martin Brian and O'Keeffe, 1978.
8 Thomas Davis, 'Our National Language', in Mark Storey (ed.), *Poetry and Ireland since 1800: A Source Book*, London, Routledge, 1988, p. 47.
9 John Williams, *Twentieth-Century British Poetry. A Critical Introduction*, London, Edward Arnold, 1987, p. 95.
10 Heaney, 1985.
11 John Hewitt, 'An Irishman in Coventry', in Frank Ormsby (ed.), *Poets from the North of Ireland*, Belfast, Blackstaff Press, 1979, p. 28.
12 Sorley Maclean, in Robin Bell(ed.), *The Best of Scottish Poetry*, Edinburgh, Chambers, 1989, p. 112.
13 Michael O'Loughlin, 'Cuchulainn', in Sebastian Barry (ed.), *The Inherited Boundaries: Younger Poets of the Republic of Ireland*, Dublin, Dolmen, 1986, p. 123.
14 John Montague, 'Like Dolmens Round My Childhood, the Old People', in Ormsby, pp. 89–90.
15 Norman MacCaig, 'Rings on a Tree' (1968), in Charles King, *Twelve Modern Scottish Poets*, London, University of London Press, 1971, p. 102.
16 John Speirs, 'A Survey of Medieval Verse', in Boris Ford (ed.), *The Age of Chaucer*, Harmondsworth, Penguin, 1954, p. 54.
17 William of Malmesbury (c.1130) cited in Bruce Dickins and R. M. Wilson (eds), *Early Middle English Texts*, London, Bowes and Bowes, 1951, p. xvii.
18 Douglas Hyde, A Literary History of Ireland, London, Benn, 1967 (first published 1899), p. 216.
19 Hyde, p. 453.

20 Hyde, p. 493.
21 *The Complaynt of Scotland* (1549), cited in Glanville Price, p. 189.
22 *The Complaynt of Scotland*, cited in Rory Watson, *The Literature of Scotland*, London, Macmillan, 1984, p. 93.
23 Parry, p. 196.
24 Michael Kelly, *Reminiscences*, vol. 1, cited in Hyde, p. 622.
25 Nicholas Phillipson, *The Enlightenment in Context*, Cambridge, Cambridge University Press, 1981, pp. 19–20.
26 Sean Lucy, 'What is Anglo-Irish Poetry?', in Sean Lucy (ed.), *Irish Poets in English*, Cork and Dublin, 1973, p. 15.
27 David Cairns and Sean Richards, *Writing Ireland: Colonialism, Nationalism and Culture*, Manchester, Manchester University Press, 1988, p. 154.
28 Siegbert Prawer, *Comparative Literary Studies: An Introduction*, London, Duckworth, 1973, p. 13.
29 Pierre Bourdieu, 'Le paradoxe du sociologue', in *Questions de sociologie*, Paris, Editions de Minuit, 1980, p. 86.
30 Patrick Kavanagh, from *Collected Prose*, 1967, in Storey, pp. 200–6.
31 Kavanagh, pp. 205–6.
32 Jackie Kay, 'Photo in the Locket', in *The Adoption Papers*, Newcastle upon Tyne, Bloodaxe Books, 1991, p. 49.
33 MacDiarmid, pp. 1170–1.
34 Alun Llewellyn-Williams, 'Here in the Quiet fields', cited in Parry, p. 431.
35 Paul Durcan, 'Ireland, 1972', in Paul Muldoon (ed.), *The Faber Book of Contemporary Irish Poetry*, London, Faber and Faber, 1986, p. 314.
36 Ian Crichton-Smith, 'Seagulls', in King, p. 172.
37 Geoffrey Hill, 'Idylls of the King', from *Tenebrae*, London, André Deutsch, 1978.
38 Anthony Thorlby, *The Times Literary Supplement*, 25 July 1968, p. 794.
39 C. D. Narasimhaiah, *The Swan and the Eagle*, Simla, Indian Institute of Advanced Study, 1969, p. 8.
40 Clayton Koelb and Susan Noakes, *The Comparative Perspective on Literature: Approaches to Theory and Practice*, New York, Cornell University Press, 1988, p. 6.
41 Koelb and Noakes, p. 6.

CHAPTER 4   COMPARATIVE IDENTITIES IN THE POST-COLONIAL WORLD

1 Peter Hulme, *Colonial Encounters, Europe and the Native Caribbean 1492–1797*, London, Routledge, 1986, pp. 49–50.

2 Edmundo O'Gorman, *La invención de America*, Mexico, FCE, 1984.
3 Carlos Fuentes, 'García Márquez and the Invention of America', in *Myself with Others, Selected Essays*, London, André Deutsch, 1988, p. 184.
4 Fuentes, p. 184.
5 Wole Soyinka, *Myth, Literature and the African World*, Cambridge, Cambridge University Press, 1976, p. vii.
6 Chidi Amuta, *The Theory of African Literature*, London, Zed Books, 1989, p. 3.
7 Ngugi Wa Thiong'O, 'On the abolition of the English Department', in *Homecoming: Essays on African and Caribbean Literature*, Culture and Politics, London, Heinemann, 1972.
8 Nadine Gordimer, *The Black Interpreters*, SPRO-CAS/RAVAN, Johannesburg, 1973, p. 5.
9 Jahnheinz Jahn, 'Die Neo-Afrikanische Literatur', *Kindles Literatur Lexicon*, p. 695, cited in James Snead, 'European Pedigrees/African Contagions: Nationality, Narrative, and Community in Tutuola, Achebe, and Reed', in Homi Bhabha (ed.) *Nation and Narration*, London, Routledge, 1990, pp. 231–49
10 Bill Ashcroft, Gareth Griffiths, Helen Tiffin, *The Empire Writes Back, Theory and Practice in Post-colonial Literatures*, London, Routledge, 1989, p. 36.
11 J. Hector St. John Crèvecoeur, *Letters from an American Farmer*, cited in Russell Reising, *The Unusable Past: Theory and the Study of American Literature*, London, Methuen, 1986.
12 Fuentes, 1988.
13 Ashcroft, *et al.*, 145.
14 George Lamming, *The Pleasures of Exile*, London, Michael Joseph, 1960, p. 3.
15 Rodolfo Gonzalez, *I am Joaquín (Yo soy Joaquín)*, Toronto, New York, London, Bantam Books, 1972, p. 1.
16 Hulme, 1986; see chapter 3, 'Prospero and Caliban', pp. 89–137.
17 Hulme, p. 128.
18 Lamming, 1960, p. 3.
19 See: unpublished doctoral thesis on Wilson Harris and García Márquez, Patricia Murray, University of Warwick, 1993.
20 Octavio Paz, *The Labyrinth of Solitude*, New York, Grove Press, 1961.
21 Gordimer, p. 5.
22 Gordimer, p. 6.
23 Soyinka, p. 127.
24 Soyinka, p. 129.

25 Gabriel García Márquez, 'The solitude of Latin America', Nobel Address, 1982, in Bernard McGuirk and Richard Caldwell (eds), *Gabriel García Márquez, New Readings*, Cambridge, Cambridge University Press, 1987, pp. 201–11.
26 Octavio Paz, 'El arquero, la flecha y el blanco', *Vuelta*, no. 117, August 1986, pp. 26–9.
27 Edward Brathwaite, 'Timehri', *Savacon* 2 (Sept, 1970), p. 42.
28 Joseph Sommers, 'Critical Approaches to Chicano Literature', in Joseph Sommers and Tomás Ybarra-Frausto (eds), *Modern Chicano Writers*, Englewood Cliffs N.J.,Prentice-Hall, 1979, pp. 31–41
29 George Lamming, quoted in interview by Raymond Gardner, *The Guardian*, 10 July 1974.

CHAPTER 5   CONSTRUCTING CULTURES: THE POLITICS OF TRAVELLERS' TALES

A version of this chapter will be appearing simultaneously in *Comparative Criticism*.

1 Michel Foucault, *The Order of Things*, London, Tavistock, 1970, p. 51.
2 Tzvetan Todorov, *La Conquête de L'Amérique: la question de l'autre*, Paris, Seuil, 1982.
3 See Peter Hulme, *Colonial Encounters*, London, Routledge, 1986; Sabina Sharkey, 'Ireland and the Iconography of Rape: Colonization, Constraint and Gender', *University of North London Occasional Papers Series*, no. 4, Sept. 1992.
4 J. B. Scott, *An Englishman at Home and Abroad 1792–1828*, Ethel Mann (ed.), 1930, pp. 76–7.
5 *A True and Faithful relation of what passed for many Yeares between Dr. John Dee, a Mathematician of Great Fame in Q. Elizabeth and K. James their Reigns, and some Spirits: Tending (had it succeeded) To a general Alteration of most States and Kingdomes in the World* . . . with Preface by Meric Casaubon, London, printed by D. Maxwell and T. Garthwaite, 1659.
6 Charlotte Fell Smith, *John Dee: 1527–1608*, London, 1909, p. 133
7 Peter French, *John Dee: The World of an Elizabethan Magus*, London, Routledge and Kegan Paul, 1972, p. 180.
8 Mary Hamer, 'Putting Ireland on the Map', *Textual Practice*, 3, no. 2, Summer 1989, pp. 184–202.
9 French, p. 8.
10 Fynes Moryson, *An Itinerary: His Ten Yeeres travels thorow Twelve Dominions*, J. Beale, London, 1617, p. 29.

11 Willie Docherty, photograph called 'The Other Side, Waterside, Derry, 1988', in Docherty, *Unknown Depths*, Belfast, FFotogallery, 1991.

12 Alexander Kinglake, *Eothen, or Traces of Travel Brought Home from the East* (first pub. 1844), Oxford, Oxford University Press, 1982, p. 7.

13 Edward Said, *Orientalism*, London, Routledge and Kegan Paul, 1978, p. 59.

14 Tacitus, *Germania*, trans. H. Mattingly, Harmondsworth, Penguin, 1948, p. 116.

15 Ernest Renan, 'What is a Nation?' (lecture originally given at the Sorbonne, March 1982) in Homi K. Bhabha (ed.), *Nation and Narration*, London, Routledge, 1990, pp. 8–23.

16 E. W. Lane, *Manners and Customs of the Modern Egyptians*, London, 1836, p. 296.

17 Richard Burton, *The Book of the Thousand Nights and a Night*, London, 1885–8, 17 vols., vol. 1, pp. 234–5.

18 Rana Kabbani, *Europe's Myths of Orient*, London, Macmillan, 1986.

19 Claudio Magris, *Danube*, trans. Patrick Creagh, London, Collins Harvill, 1990, p. 29.

20 William Morris, *Journals of Travel in Iceland. The Collected Works of William Morris*, vol. 8, New York, Russell and Russell, 1966, pp. xxxiii–xxxiv.

21 Morris, pp. 139 and 239.

22 William Morris, *The Novel on Blue Paper*, Penelope Fitzgerald (ed.), London and West Nyack, The Journeyman Press, 1982.

23 Morris, 1982, p. 70.

24 W. H. Auden and Louis MacNeice, *Letters from Iceland*, Faber and Faber, 1937, p. 119.

25 Auden and MacNeice, pp. 128–9.

26 Kinglake, pp. 36–7.

27 *The Complete Letters of Lady Mary Wortley Montagu*, Robert Halsband (ed.), vol. 1, 1708–20, Oxford, The Clarendon Press, 1965, p. 383.

28 Paul Rycaut, *The Present State of the Ottoman Empire*, London, J. Starkey and H. Brome, 1668.

29 Montague, p. 408.

30 Said, p. 20.

31 Sara Mills, *Discourses of Difference: An Analysis of Women's Travel Writing and Colonialism*, London, Routledge, 1991, p. 63.

32 Julia Pardoe, *Beauties of the Bosphorus*, London, George Virtue, 1838.

33 Kinglake, pp. 32–3.
34 Mills, p. 121.
35 Mills, p. 199.

CHAPTER 6   GENDER AND THEMATICS: A CASE STUDY

1 Clayton Koelb and Susan Noakes, (eds), *The Comparative Perspective on Literature*, Ithaca, Cornell University Press, 1988.
2 René Wellek, 'The Name and Nature of Comparative Literature', *Discriminations*, New Haven, Yale University Press, 1970, p.19.
3 Siegbert Prawer, *Comparative Literary Studies: an Introduction*, London, Duckworth, 1973. See chapter 6, 'Themes and Prefigurations', pp. 99–114.
4 Raymond Trousson, *Un Problème de littérature comparée; les études de thémes*, Paris, 1965.
5 Prawer, p. 102.
6 Elaine Showalter, *The New Feminist Criticism*, London, Virago, 1986, p. 5.
7 Showalter, p. 7.
8 Adrienne Rich, *Of Woman Born: Motherhood as Experience and Institution*, London, Virago, 1977.
9 T. H. White, *The Once and Future King*, London, Fontana, 1958. All references are to this edition. Gillian Bradshaw, *Down the Long Wind*, London, Methuen, 1984. All references are to this edition.
10 Alfred Tennyson, *Idylls of the King*, in *The Works of Tennyson*, London, Macmillan, 1907. All citations from this edition.
11 Norris J. Lacey and Geoffrey Ashe, *The Arthurian Handbook*, London and New York, Garland, 1988.
12 Mary Condren, *The Serpent and the Goddess, Women, Religion and Power in Celtic Ireland*, New York, Harper and Row, 1989, p. 25.
13 Condren, p.43
14 Thomas Mallory, *Le Morte d'Arthur*, 2 vols, Harmondsworth, Penguin 1986; vol. 1, p. 194. All references are to this edition.
15 Mallory, vol. 2, p. 426.
16 Mallory, vol. 2, p. 458.
17 White, p. 541.
18 White, pp. 626–7.
19 Stephen Greenblatt, *Learning to Curse: Essays in Early Modern Culture*, London and New York, Routledge, 1990, p. 170.
20 Roger Ascham, *The Scholemaster*. London, John Daye, 1570.
21 Catherine Belsey, *The Subject of Tragedy: Identity and Difference in Renaissance Drama*, London, Methuen, 1985, p.194.

22   Leodogran, the King of Cameliard
            Had one fair daughter, and none other child;
            And she was fairest of all flesh on earth,
            Guinevere, and in her his one delight.

23 Françoise Barret-Ducrocq, *Love in the Time of Victoria*, London, Verso, 1991.

24 William Morris, 'The Defence of Guinevere', in *The Works of William Morris*, ed. with prefaces by May Morris, 24 vols, London, Longmans Green, 1910–15.

25 Mario Praz, *The Romantic Agony*, Oxford, Clarendon Press, 1933.

26 Prawer, p. 101.

27 H. R. Jauss, 'Literary History as a Challenge to Literary Theory', *New Literary History*, no 2, 1970, pp. 11–19.

28 See: *The Princess: A Medley, The Works of Alfred, Lord Tennyson*, London, Macmillan, 1907, pp. 165–218.

CHAPTER 7   FROM COMPARATIVE LITERATURE TO TRANSLATION STUDIES

1 Hilaire Belloc, *On Translation*, Oxford, Clarendon Press, 1931.

2 Itamar Evan-Zohar, 'Translation Theory Today', *Poetics Today*, 2, no. 4. Summer/Autumn 1981, pp. 1–7.

3 Lori Chamberlain, 'Gender and the Metaphorics of Translation', in Lawrence Venuti(ed.), *Rethinking Translation*, London, Routledge, 1992, pp. 57–74.

4 Barbara Johnson, 'The Surprise of Otherness: A Note on the Wartime Writings of Paul de Man', in Peter Collier and Helga Geyer-Ryan (eds), *Literary Theory Today*, London, Polity Press, 1990 pp. 13–23.

5 Itamar Evan-Zohar, 'The Position of Translated Literature within the Literary Polysystem', *Papers in Historical Poetics*, Tel Aviv, 1978.

6 Maria Tymoczko, 'Translation as a force for literary revolution in the twelfth century: the shift from epic to romance', *New Comparison*, no. 1, Summer 1986, pp. 7–27.

7 Lawrence Venuti (ed.), *Rethinking Translation: Discourse, Subjectivity, Ideology*, London, Routledge, 1992, pp. 5–6.

8 Vladimír Macura, 'Culture as Translation', in Susan Bassnett and André Lefevere(eds), *Translation, History and Culture*, London, Pinter, 1990, pp. 64–70.

9 José Lambert and Rik Van Gorp, 'On describing translations', in Theo Hermans(ed.), *The Manipulation of Literature*, London, Croom Helm, 1985, pp. 42–53.

10 Edward Sapir, *Culture, Language and Personality*, Berkeley, Los Angeles, University of California Press, 1956, p. 69.

11 Theo Hermans, 'Images of Translation: Metaphor and Imagery in the Renaissance Discourse on Translation', in *The Manipulation of Literature*, pp. 103–35.

12 Perrot d'Ablancourt, preface to the *Annals of Tacitus*, in *Lettres et Préfaces critiques*, Roger Zuber(ed.), Paris, 1972.

13 John Dryden, Dedication to *The Aeneid*, 1697, in *Of Dramatic Poesy and Other Critical Essays*, G. Watson (ed.), 2 vols, London/New York, Dent/Dutton, 1962.

14 Madame de Gournay,*Versions de quelques piéces de Virgile*, Paris, 1619.

15 Michel Foucault, *The Order of Things*, London, Tavistock, 1970, p. 43.

16 André Lefevere, 'What Is Written Must Be Rewritten, Julius Caesar: Shakespeare, Voltaire, Wieland, Buckingham', in Theo Hermans (ed.), *Second Hand: Papers on the Theory and Historical Study of Literary Translation*, Antwep, ALW-Cahier no. 3, 1985, pp. 88–106.

17 See Armin Paul Frank, 'Translation Anthologies: An Invitation to the Curious and a Case Study', *Target* 3:1, 1991, pp. 65–90; Harald Kittel and Armin Paul Frank (eds), *Interculturality and the Historical Study of Literary Translations*, Erich Schmidt Verlag, Berlin, 1991.

18 André Lefevere, 'Translation Studies: The Goal of the Discipline', in J. Holmes, J. Lambert and A. Lefevere (eds), *Literature and Translation*, Leuven, ACCO, 1978, pp. 234–5.

19 Susan Bassnett and André Lefevere (eds), *Translation, History and Culture*, London, Pinter, 1990, p. 12.

20 John Dryden, Preface to the *Life of Lucian*, 1711, in G. Watson (ed.).

21 Ezra Pound, Letter to Iris Barry, 20 July 1916, in D. D. Paige (ed.), *The Letters of Ezra Pound 1907–1916*, London, Faber and Faber, 1961.

22 Ezra Pound, Letter to A. R. Orage, April 1916, in Paige, (ed.).

23 Jacques Derrida, 'Des Tours de Babel', in Joseph F. Graham (ed.), *Difference in Translation*, Ithaca, Cornell University Press, 1985.

24 Walter Benjamin, 'The Task of the Translator', in *Illuminations*, London, Fontana, 1973, pp. 69–83.

25 See Andrew Benjamin, *Translation and the Nature of Philosophy*, London, Routledge, 1990.

26 See: Roger Ellis (ed.) *The Medieval Translator*, vol. 1, Woodbridge, D. S. Brewer, 1989; Roger Ellis (ed.) *Translation in the Middle Ages*, *New Comparison* 12, Autumn 1991.

27 Bill Ashcroft, Gareth Griffiths, Helen Tiffin, *The Empire Writes Back*, London, Routledge, 1989, pp. 195–6.

28 See: Else Veira, *Por uma teoria pos-moderna da traduçao*, unpublished PhD thesis, University of Minas Gerais, The first chapter of

this thesis was presented as a doctoral seminar paper in the Graduate School of Comparative Literary Theory and Translation Studies at the University of Warwick. I am immeasurably grateful to Else Veira for introducing me to the work of Brazilian translation theorists.

29 Oswald de Andrade, *Manifesto Antropófago*, in A. Candido and J. A. Castellor, *Presençã da Literatura Brasiliera*, vol. III, *Modernismo*, São Paolo, Difusão Européia do Livro, 1968, pp. 68–74.

30 Randal Johnson, 'Tupy or not Tupy: Cannibalism and Nationalism in Contemporary Brazilian Literature', in John King (ed.), *Modern Latin American fiction: A Survey*, London, Faber and Faber, 1987, pp. 41–59.

31 Again I am grateful to Else Veira for pointing this out to me.

32 Veira, as above.

33 Haraldo de Campos, *Deus e o diabo no Fausto de Goethe*, Sao Paulo, Perspectiva, 1981. See also 'Mephistofaustian Transluciferation', in *Dispositio*, vol. 7, nos 19, 20, 21, 1982, pp. 42–60.

34 De Campos, p. 208.

35 Veira, as above.

36 Hélène Cixous, 'La Rire de la Méduse', *L'Arc* 61, 1975, pp. 39–54, English translation by Keith and Paula Cohen, 'The Laugh of the Medusa', *Signs*, I, Summer 1976, pp. 875–99.

37 Nicole Ward-Jouve, 'To fly/to steal; no more? Translating French feminisms into English', in *White Woman Speaks with Forked Tongue: Criticism as Autobiography*, London, Routledge, 1991, p. 47.

38 Kathy Mezei, 'The Reader and the decline...'*Tessera: L'Écriture comme Lecture*, September, 1985, pp. 21–31.

39 George Steiner, *After Babel*, London and New York, Oxford University Press, 1975.

40 Barbara Godard, 'Theorizing Feminist Discourse/Translation', in Bassnett and Lefevere (eds), pp. 89–96.

41 Suzanne de Lotbinière-Harwood, 'About the *her* in other', Preface to Lise Gauvin, *Letters from An Other*, Toronto, Women's Press, 1989, p. 9.

42 Henri Meschonnic, 'Propositions pour une poétique de la traduction', in *Pour la Poétique*, vol. II, Paris, 1973, p. 308.

43 André Lefevere, *Translation/History/Culture: A Source Book*, London, Routledge, 1992. p. 2.

44 Bassnett and Lefevere, p. 12.

45 Heidi Hartmann, 'The Unhappy Marriage of Marxism and Feminism: Towards a More Progressive Union', in Lydia Sargent (ed.) *Women and Revolution*, London, Pluto Press, 1981, pp. 1–42.

Select Bibliography

The purpose of this bibliography is to provide an introduction to the three main areas of research that underpin this book: monographs and collections of essays on aspects of comparative literature and literary theory; works collected under the general heading of post-colonial theory; works in the field of translation studies. Many of these books contain useful bibliographies.

COMPARATIVE LITERATURE: GENERAL INTRODUCTORY

Aldridge, A. Owen, (ed.), *Comparative Literature: Matter and Method*, Urbana, University of Illinois Press, 1964.

Brandt-Corstius, Jan, *Introduction to the Comparative Study of Literature*, New York, 1967.

Collier, Peter and Geyer-Ryan, Helga, *Literary Theory Today*, London, Polity, 1990.

Deeney, John, *Comparative Literature from Chinese Perspectives*, Shenyang, Liaoning University Press, 1990.

Eagleton, Terry, *Literary Theory: An Introduction*, Oxford, Blackwell, 1983.

Etiemble, René, *Comparaison n'est pas raison: la Crise de la littérature comparée*, Paris, Gallimard, 1967.

Gifford, Henry, *Comparative Literature*, London, 1969.

Guillen, Claudio, *Entre lo uno y lo diverso: Introducción a la literatura comparada*, Barcelona, Editorial Critica, 1985.

Guyard, Marius-François, *La Littérature comparée*, Paris, 1951.

Harari, J. V., (ed.), *Textual Strategies: Perspectives in Postmodernist Criticism*, London, Methuen, 1980.

Jefferson, A. and Robey, D., (eds), *Modern Literary Theory: A Com-*

parative Introduction, London, Batsford, 1982.

Jost, François, *Introduction to Comparative Literature*, Indianapolis, Bobbs-Merrill, 1974.

Koelb, Clayton and Noakes, Susan, (eds), *The Comparative Perspective on Literature. Approaches to Theory and Practice*, Ithaca and London, Cornell University Press, 1988.

Lefevere, André, *Translation, Rewriting and the Manipulation of Literary Fame*, London, Routledge, 1992.

Levin, Harry, *Refractions. Essays in Comparative Literature*, Oxford, 1972.

Majumdar, Swapan, *Comparative Literature, Indian Dimensions*, Calcutta, Papyrus, 1987.

Nicholls Jr., Stephen G. and Vowles, Richard B, (eds), *Comparatists at Work: Studies in Comparative Literature*, Waltham, Mass., Blaisdell, 1968.

Pichois, C. and Rousseau, André-M., *La littérature comparée*, Paris, 1967.

Porta, Antonio, *La letteratura comparata nella storia e nella critica*, Milan, Mondadori, 1951.

Prawer, Siegbert, *Comparative Literary Studies: an Introduction*, London, Duckworth, 1973.

Rice, Philip and Waugh, Patricia, (eds), *Modern Literary Theory: A Reader*, London, Edward Arnold, 1989.

Schultz, H. J. and Rhein, P. H., (eds), *Comparative Literature: The Early Years*, Chapel Hill, University of North Carolina Press, 1973.

Stallknecht, N. P. (ed.), *Comparative Literature: Method and Perspective*, Carbondale, Southern Illinois University Press, 1961.

Van Tieghem, Paul, *La Littérature comparée*, Paris, Colin, 1951.

Warren, Austin and Wellek, René, *Theory of Literature*, New York, Harvest, 1968.

Weisstein, Ulrich, *Comparative Literature and Literary Theory*, Bloomington, Indiana University Press, 1974. This book contains a useful bibliography.

Wellek, René, *Concepts of Criticism*, New Haven, Yale University Press, 1963.

Wellek, René, *Discriminations: Further Concepts of Criticism*, New Haven, Yale University Press, 1970.

Wrenn, C. L., *The Idea of Comparative Literature*, London, Modern Humanities Research Association, 1968.

Zhouhan, Yang and Daiyun, Yue, Literatures, *Histories and Literary Histories*, Shenyang, Liaoning University Press, 1989.

Useful periodicals:
Revue de littérature comparée 1921–

Comparative Literature 1949–
Comparative Literature Studies 1943–
Yearbook of Comparative and General Literature 1952–
Comparative Criticism 1979–
New Comparison 1986–

POST-COLONIAL THEORY

Amuta, Chidi, *The Theory of African Literature*, London, Zed Books, 1989.

Ashcroft, Bill, Griffiths, Gareth and Tiffin, Helen, *The Empire Writes Back: Theory and Practice in Post-Colonial Literatures*, London, Routledge, 1989. This book contains a useful bibliography.

Balibar, Etienne and Wallerstein, I., *Race, Nation, Class: Ambiguous Identities*, London, Verso, 1988.

Bhabha, H., (ed), *Nation and Narration*, London Routledge, 1990.

Bitterlee, U. *Cultures in Conflict: Encounters Between Europe and non-European Cultures 1492–1800*, London, Polity, 1986.

Calderon, H. and Saldivar, J. D., (eds), *Criticism in the Borderlands: Studies in Chicano Literature, Culture and Ideology*, Durham, North Carolina, Duke University Press, 1990.

Cheyfitz, E. *The Poetics of Imperialism: Translation and Colonization from the Tempest to Tarzan*, New York and Oxford, Oxford University Press, 1991.

Crabb, P., (ed.), *Theory and Practice in Comparative Studies: Canada, Australia and New Zealand*, Sydney, AMSACZ, 1983.

Fanon, F., *Studies in a Dying Colonialism*, Harmondsworth, Penguin, 1959.

Fanon, F., *The Wretched of the Earth*, Harmondsworth, Penguin, 1961.

Fanon, F., *Black Skin, White Masks*, New York, Grove Press, 1967.

Gates Jr., Henry Louis, (ed.), *Black Literature and Literary Theory*, London and New York, Methuen, 1984.

Gates Jr., Henry Louis, *"Race", Writing and Difference*, Chicago, University of Chicago Press, 1986.

Fuentes, Carlos, *Myself and Others: Selected Essays*, London, André Deutsch, 1988.

Griffiths, Gareth, *A Double Exile: African and West Indian Writing Between Two Cultures*, London, Marion Boyars, 1978.

Harasym, S., (ed.), *Gayatri Spivak: The Post-colonial Critic. Interviews, Strategies, Dialogues*, London, Routledge, 1987.

Harris, Wilson, *Explorations: A Selection of Talks and Articles, 1966–1981*, ed. Hena Maes-Jelinek, Aarhus, Dangaroo, 1981.

Harris, Wilson, *The Womb of Space: The Cross-Cultural Imagination*, Westport Connecticut, Greenwood, 1983.

Holst-Petersen, K. and Rutherford, A., (eds), *A Double Colonialization: Colonial and Post-Colonial Women's Writing*, Aarhus, Dangaroo, 1985.

Hulme, Peter, *Colonial Encounters*, London, Routledge, 1986.

Hyam, R., *Empire and Sexuality: The British Experience*, Manchester, Manchester University Press, 1990.

Janmohammed, A., *Manichean Aesthetics: The Politics of Literature in Colonial Africa*, Amherst, University of Massachussetts Press, 1983.

Lamming, George, *The Pleasures of Exile*, London, Michael Joseph, 1980.

Lazarus, N., *Resistance in Post-Colonial African Fiction*, New Haven and London, Yale University Press, 1990.

McDougall, R. and Whitlock, G., *Australian/Canadian Literatures in English: Comparative Perspectives*, North Ryde, Methuen, 1987.

Mahood, M. M., *The Colonial Encounter*, London, Rex Collings, 1977.

Mannoni, O., *Prospero and Caliban: The Psychology of Colonization*, New York, Praeger, 1964.

Mills, Sara, *Discourses of Difference: An Analysis of Women's Travel Writing and Colonialism*, London, Routledge, 1991.

Minh-ha, T. T., *Women, Native, Other: Writing, Postcoloniality and Feminism*, Bloomington, Indiana University Press, 1989.

Ngugi wa Thiong'o, *Homecoming: Essays on African and Caribbean Literature*, Culture and Politics, London, Heinemann, 1972.

Ngugi wa Thiong'o, *Decolonising the Mind: the Politics of Language in African Literature*, London, Currey, 1986.

Ridley, Hugh, *Images of Imperial Rule*, London, Croom Helm, 1983.

Said, E., *Orientalism*, New York, Pantheon, 1978.

Said, E., *The World, the Text and the Critic*, London, Faber, 1984.

Said, E., *Culture and Imperialism*, London, Chatto and Windus, 1993.

Soyinka, Wole, *Myth, Literature and the African World*, Cambridge, Cambridge University Press, 1976.

Sommers, J. and Ybarra-Frausto, T., *Modern Chicano Writers*, Englewood Cliffs, N. J., Prentice-Hall, 1979.

Spivak, G., *In Other Worlds: Essays in Cultural Politics*, London, Methuen, 1987.

Young, Robert, *White Mythologies: Writing, History and the West*, London, Routledge, 1990.

TRANSLATION STUDIES

Arrowsmith, W. and Shattuck, R., (eds), *The Craft and Context of Translation*, Austin, University of Texas Press, 1961.

Bassnett-McGuire, Susan, *Translation Studies*, revised edn, London, Routledge, 1991. first Publ. 1980.

Bassnett, S. and Lefevere, A., *Translation, History and Culture*, London, Pinter, 1990.

Brower, Reuben, (ed.), *On Translation*, Cambridge, Mass., Harvard University Press, 1959.

De Beaugrande, Robert, *Text, Discourse and Process*, London, Longman, 1980.

Benjamin, Andrew, *Translation and the Nature of Philosophy*, London, Routledge, 1989.

Berman, Antoine, *Les Tours de Babel: Essais sur la traduction*, Maurezin, Editions Trans-Europ-Repress, 1985.

Biguenet, John and Schulte, Rainer, (eds), *The Craft of Translation*, Chicago, University of Chicago Press, 1989.

Bly, Robert, *The Eight Stages of Translation*, Boston, Rowan Tree Press, 1983.

Catford, J. C., *A Linguistic Theory of Translation*, London, Oxford University Press, 1965.

Delisle, Jean, Translation: *An Interpretive Approach*, Ottawa and London, University of Ottawa Press, 1988.

Evan-Zohar, Itamar, *Papers in Historical Poetics*, Tel Aviv, The Porter Institute for Poetics and Semiotics, 1978.

Gaddis Rose, M., (ed.), *Translation Spectrum: Essays in Theory and Practice*, Albany, State University of New York, 1981.

Gentzler, E., *Contemporary Translation Theories*, London, Routledge, 1993.

Graham, J. F., *Difference and Translation*, Ithaca and London, Cornell University Press, 1985.

Hatim, Basil and Mason, Ian, *Discourse and Translation*, London, Longman, 1990.

Heylen, Romy, *Translation, Poetics and the Stage: Six French Hamlets*, London, Routledge, 1993.

Hermans, Theo, (ed.), *The Manipulation of Literature*, London, Croom Helm, 1985.

Holmes, J., (ed.), *The Nature of Translation: Essays on the Theory and Practice of Literary Translation*, The Hague, Mouton, 1970.

Holmes, James, Lambert, J. and Lefevere, A., (eds), *Literature and Translation*, Louvain, ACCO, 1978.

Holmes, J., *Translated! Papers on Literary Translation and Translation Studies*, Amsterdam, Rodopi, 1988.

Kelly, L. G., *The True Interpreter: A History of Translation Theory and Practice in the West*, Oxford, Blackwell, 1979.

Kittel, Harald and Frank, Armin Paul, *Interculturality and the Historical*

Study of Literary Translation, Berlin, Erich Schmidt Verlag, 1991.

Lefevere, A., *Translating Poetry: Seven Strategies and a Blueprint*, Assen and Amsterdam, Van Gorcum, 1975.

Lefevere, A., (ed.), *Translation/History/Culture: A Sourcebook*, London, Routledge, 1992.

Lefevere, A., *Translation, Rewriting and the Manipulation of Literary Fame*, London, Routledge, 1992.

Newmark, Peter, *Approaches to Translation*, London, Pergamon, 1981.

Newmark, Peter, *A Textbook of Translation*, London, Prentice-Hall, 1988.

Nida, Eugene, *Towards a Science of Translating*, Leiden, E. J. Brill, 1964.

Nida, Eugene and Taber, E., *The Theory and Practice of Translating*, Leiden, E. J. Brill, 1969.

Schulte, Rainer and Biguenet, John, (eds), *Theories of Translation. An Anthology of Essays from Dryden to Derrida*, Chicago, University of Chicago Press, 1992.

Scolnicova, Hanna and Holland, Peter, (eds), *The Play out of Context: Transferring Plays from Culture to Culture*, Cambridge, Cambridge University Press, 1989.

Snell-Hornby, Mary, *Translation Studies: An Integrated Approach*, Amsterdam, John Benjamin, 1988.

Steiner, George, *After Babel. Aspects of Language and Translation*, London, Oxford University Press, 1975.

Steiner, T. R., *English Translation Theory 1650–1800*, Amsterdam and Assen, Van Gorcum, 1975.

Toury, Gideon, *In Search of a Theory of Translation*, Tel Aviv, The Porter Institute for Poetics and Semiotics, 1980.

Venuti, Lawrence, *Rethinking Translation. Discourse, Subjectivity, Ideology*, London, Routledge, 1992.

Warren, Rosanna, *The Art of Translation: Voices from the Field*, Boston, Northeastern University Press, 1989.

Weissbort, Daniel, (ed.), *Translating Poetry: The Double Labyrinth*, Iowa City, University of Iowa Press, 1989.

Wilss, W., *Translation Theory and its Implementation*, Tübingen, Narr, 1984.

Wollin, Hans and Lindquist, Hans., (eds), *Translation Studies in Scandinavia*, Lund, CWK Gleerup, 1986.

Zlateva, P., *Translation as Social Action*, London, Routledge, 1993.

Zuber, Ortrun, (ed.), *The Languages of the Theatre: Problems in the Translation and Transposition of Drama*, London, Pergamon, 1980.

Zuber-Skerritt, Ortrun, (ed.), *Page to Stage: Theatre as Translation*, Amsterdam, Rodopi, 1984.

Index